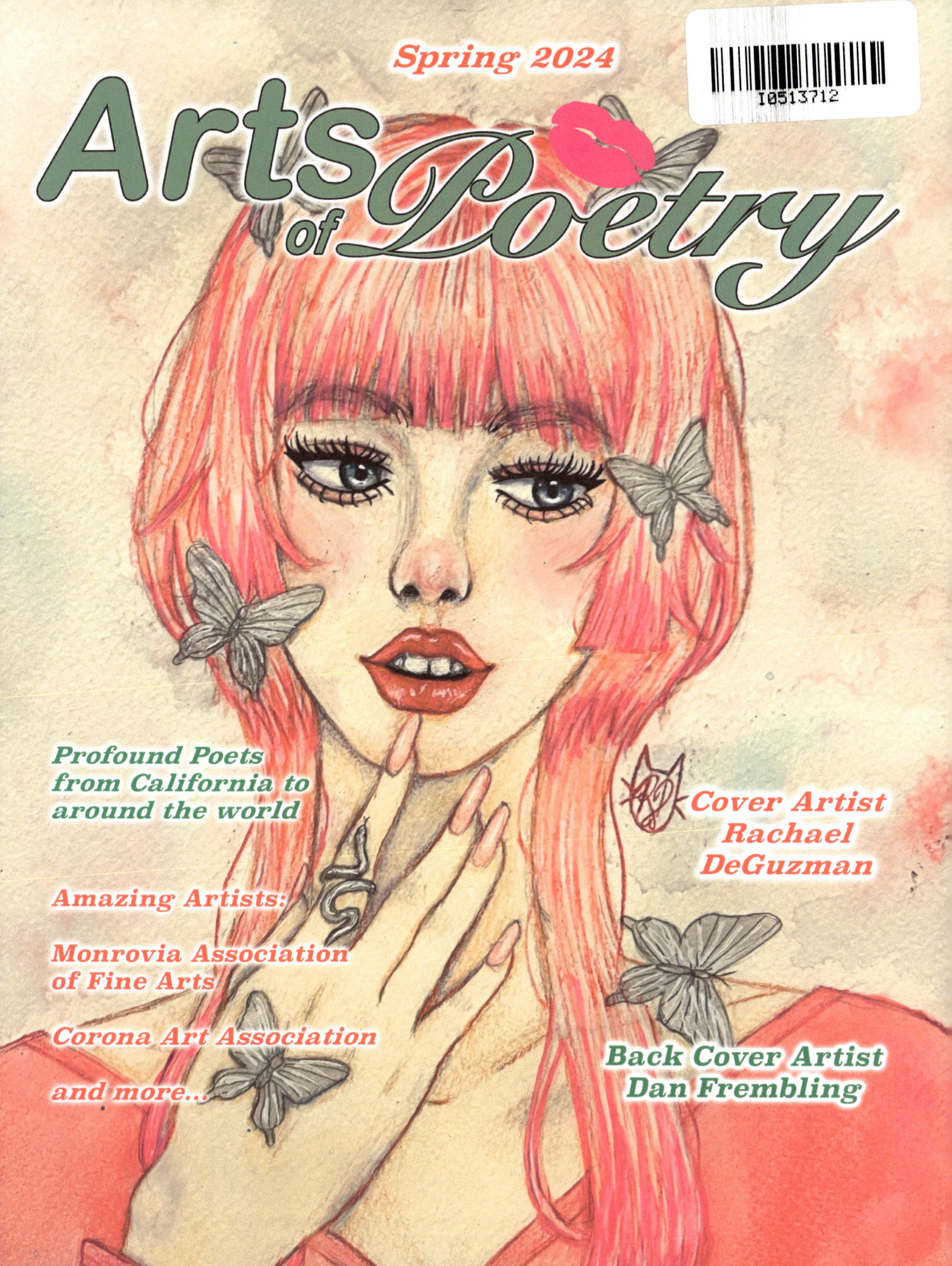

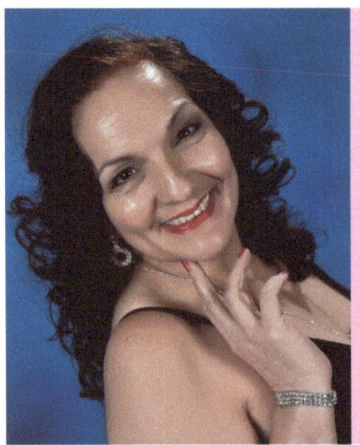

*Art is a talent not seen until it is created.
Everything needed is within the
individual artist or writer.
It comes from within our core and
is expressed as we create.
Our vision and goal is to share the beauty
of a culture that unless we as a community
embrace it would be lost forever. Unseen.
Denise Toro - Arts of Poetry*

Table of Contents
Front Cover Artist
Rachael DeGuzman
16 & 17
Back Cover Artist
Dan Frembling

MEET OUR ARTISTS

Kannan Spartan 2
Rachel Toro..3
Joan Whitenack..4
M.A. Havens...5
Corona Art Association........................6 & 7
Crystal Miao, Sonia Sleeger, Bruce Logan,
Laureen Pedroza, Alex Alarcon, Lori Alarcon,
Mary Lou Wallace, Lani Britain,
Janet Griffith, Kim Mabon, Becky Floyd
Dalton Morgan..9
Ben H Diaz..10 & 11
Laureen Pedroza,..12
Keith Slover 13
Square i Gallery ....14 & 15
Nada Fakhreddine................................20 & 21
Andrea Willow....................................22 & 23
Marc Shapiro..24
PSW -Pamela Wagstaff.............................25
Ginger Lai..26-27
Jim Balderrama...28
Dan Frembling....................................29 & 30

MEET OUR POETS
Joan Whitenack..4
M.A. Havens...5
Kevin & Melony Killoren.............................8
Carol Mae...12
Denise Toro..12
DrBendetta Perry..18
Alicia Wyneken...20
Karen Fincher...22
Marc Shapiro..24

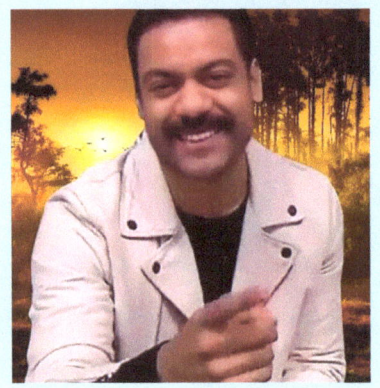

KANNAN SPARTAN

**THERE IS NO FAILURE, EITHER
ONE WINS OR ONE LEARNS**
*Cartooning
Studied at Indian Community School Kuwait
Went to Indian School Kuwait
Lives in Kuwait City
Facebook: Kannan Spartan*

Board Members
President — **Vice-President**
Founder/ Publisher — **Treasurer**
Denise Toro — Angelina Grigsby
Editor — **Secretary**
Jeana Brashier — Maria Martinez

Arts of Poetry is a 501c3 Corporation
All rights reserved. No part of this publication may be reproduced. Copyright 2018

213-373-4361 - www.artsofpoetry.com - artsofpoetry@gmail.com

Moon and Stars

Rachel Toro - Bling Bling
Personalized cups, hats and more

Rachel started her artist venture making gifts for friends and family. Now she is being asked to make special personalized gifts from her friend's friends and family. Life is an amazing journey. When you add a little bling it makes it outstanding.
Order your bling today contact moonandstarslight24@gmail.com

213-373-4361 - www.artsofpoetry.com - artsofpoetry@gmail.com

Joan Whitenack

Joan painted her very first picture at the age of 71 years just after retiring. Now, Joan loves to paint with oil paints on canvas and travel – since retiring in 2012, she has done a lot of both. She will tell you that painting is a spiritual experience and a way to share love with friends and family. She enjoys capturing the natural light, color and the beauty of our amazing world on her canvasses. She often paints landscapes and scenes from her travels thus making a memory become meaningful art.
https://www.joanwhitenack.com

Surfrider Oceanside

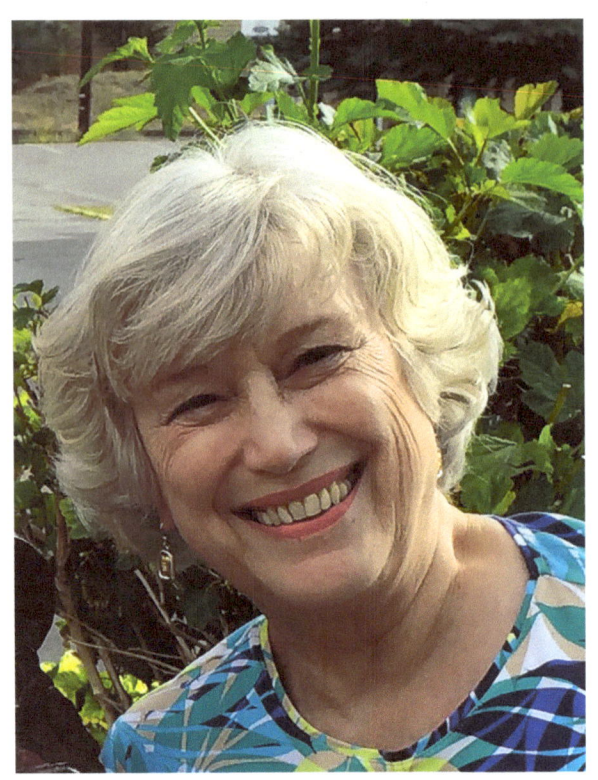

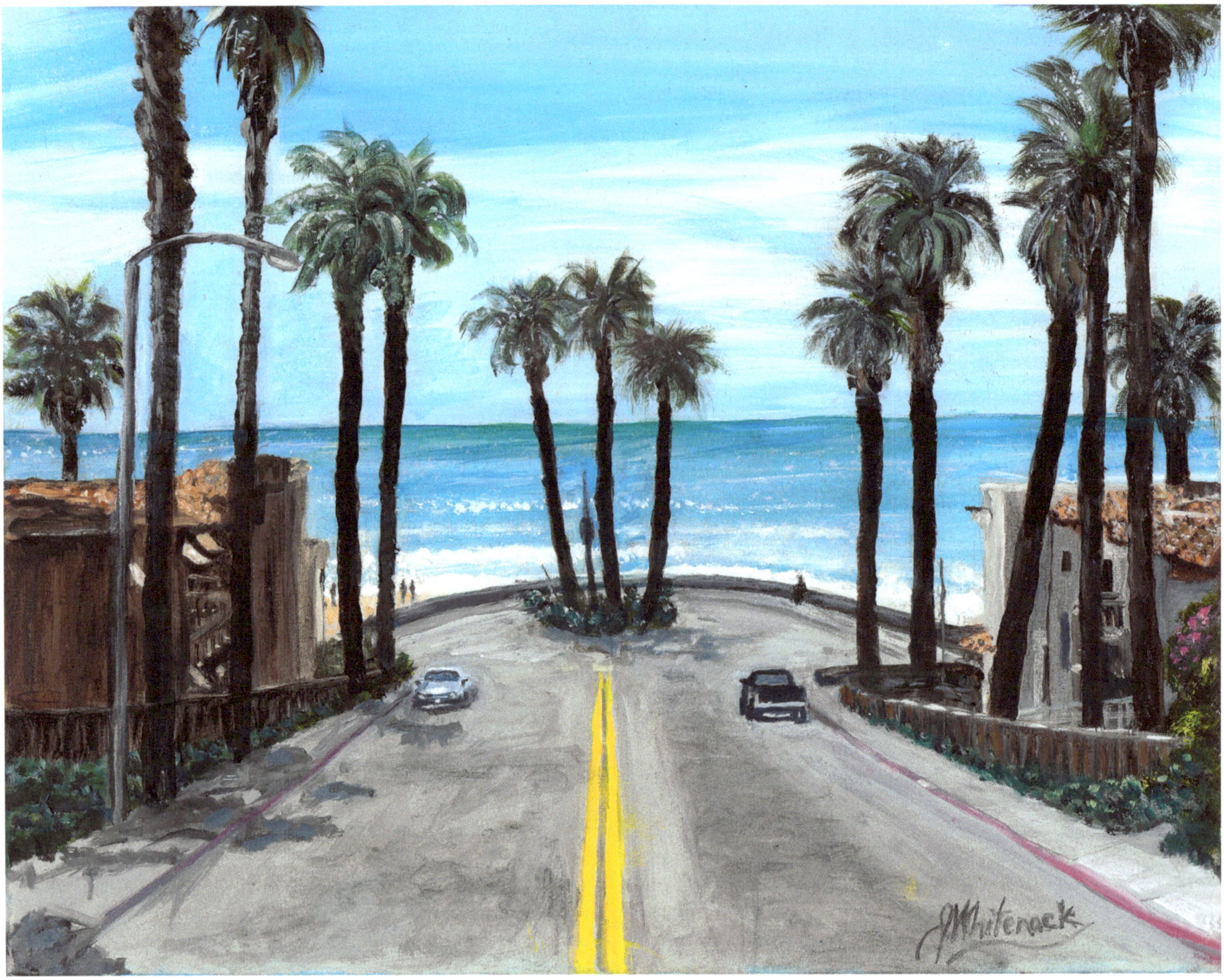

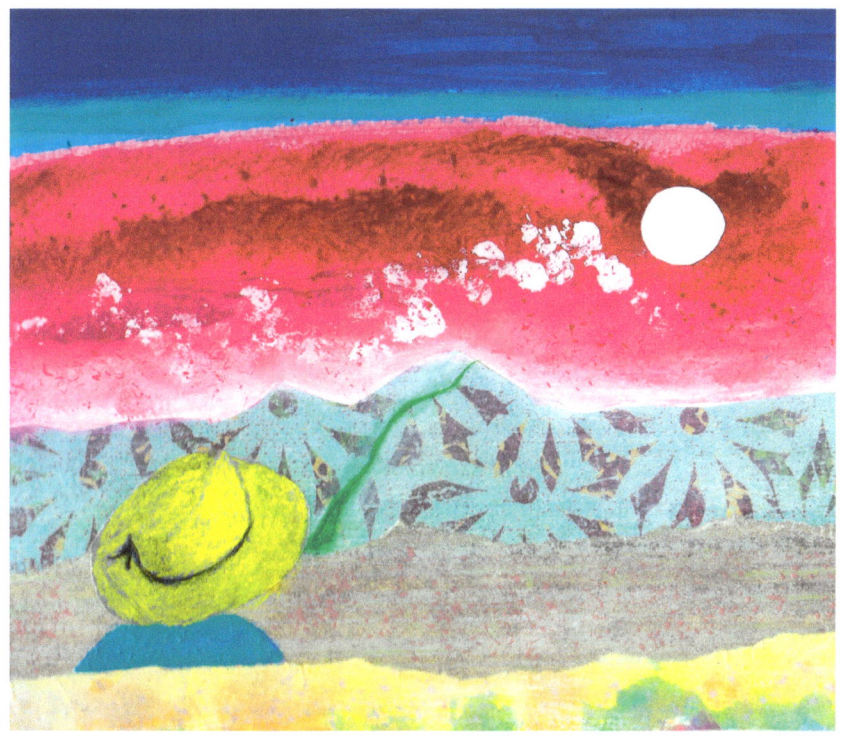

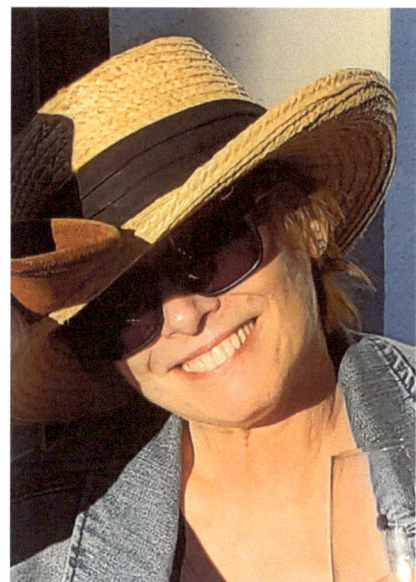

M.A. Havens
Artist & Poet

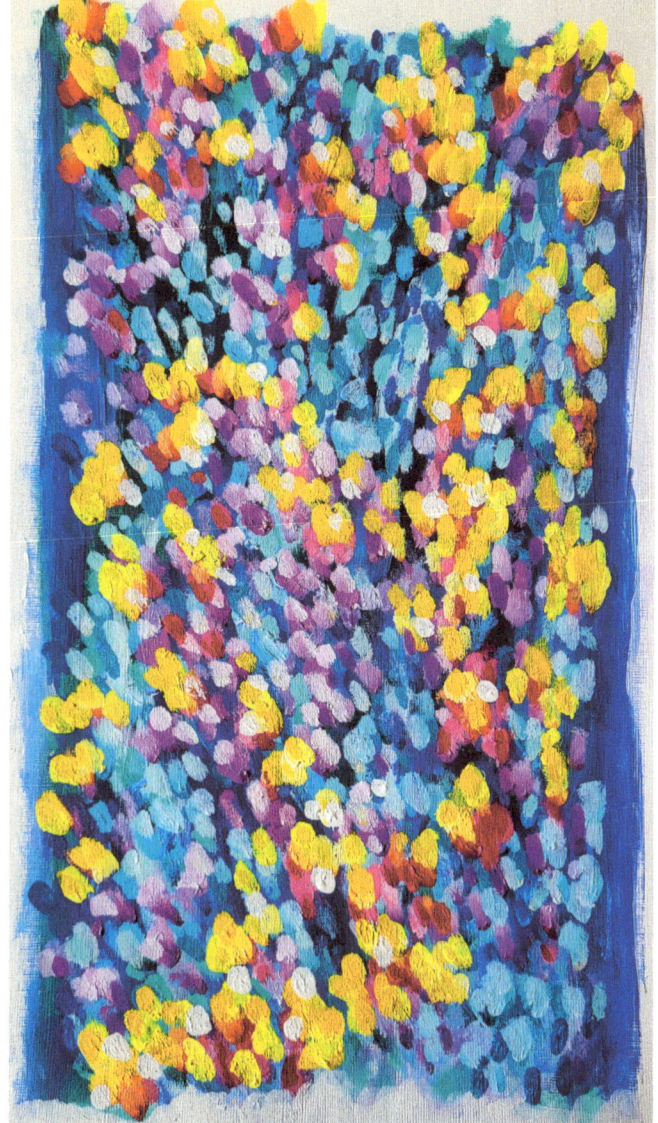

SNOWSHINE

Chilly this morning
I sip coffee at the pier
Know I have to go

And so say goodbye
To the deep blue Pacific
I crave solitude

And soon drive away
To reach freeway heading north
Treasuring silence

As the hours pass by
I seek high country refuge
That will energize

The mountains beckon
They draw and inspire me
Their vistas unfold

I continue on
Where sun rays and falling snow
Merge into Snowshine

Glistening crystals
Multicolored swirls of light
Dance and surround me

Make my spirits soar
Majesty uplifts my heart
And I have found home

SUMMER DELIGHTS

The morning sunshine
Streams through wide-open windows
I hum and I smile

Fragrant flowers bloom
From lush fields and rolling hills
Make me gasp with joy

White jasmine bushes
Sweet lilies of the valley
Like vanilla peach

Julia Child rose
Bushy buttery yellow
Subtle anise smell

Red Mister Lincoln
The rose that entrances me
Robust damask scent

Purple petunias
French lavender and bluebells
Sumptuous colors

Captivate my vision
Summertime's enchanting charm
Sets my soul aglow

written by M.A. Havens
mahavens127@gmail.com https://mahavensart.com/

213-373-4361 - www.artsofpoetry.com - artsofpoetry@gmail.com

Corona Art Association Artists

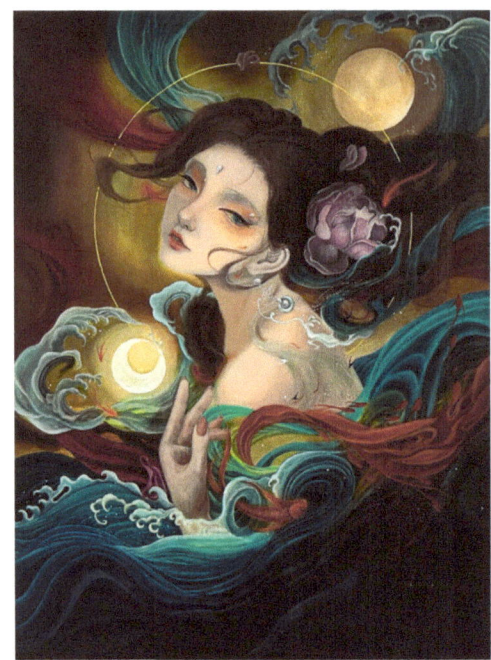
Crystal Miao

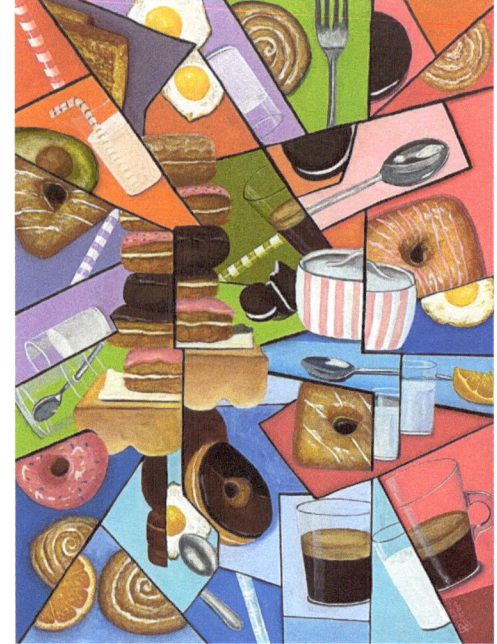
Laureen Pedroza

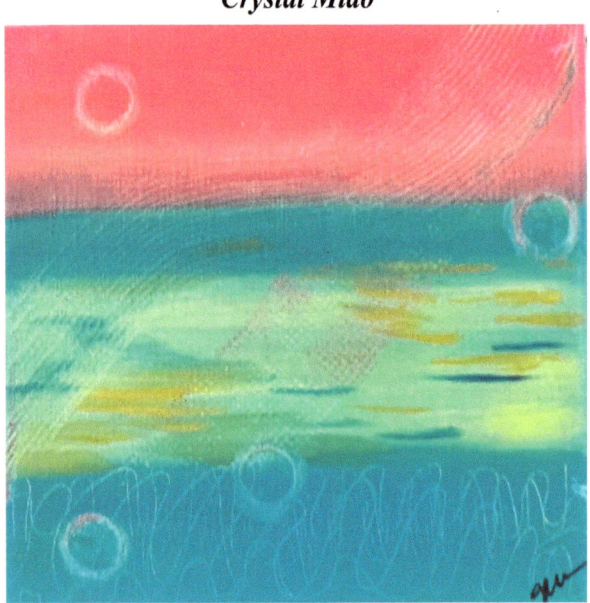
Sonia Sleeger

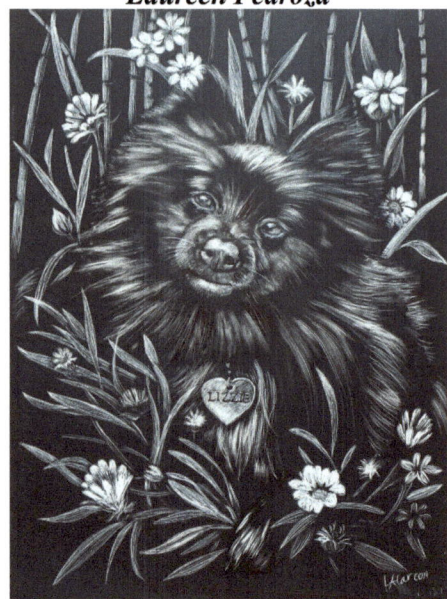
Lori Alarcon

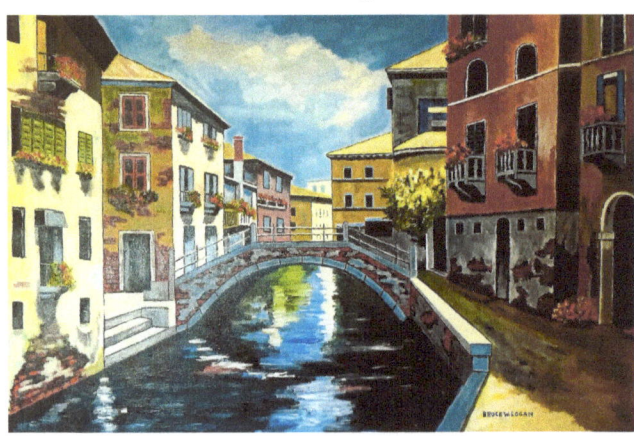
Bruce Logan

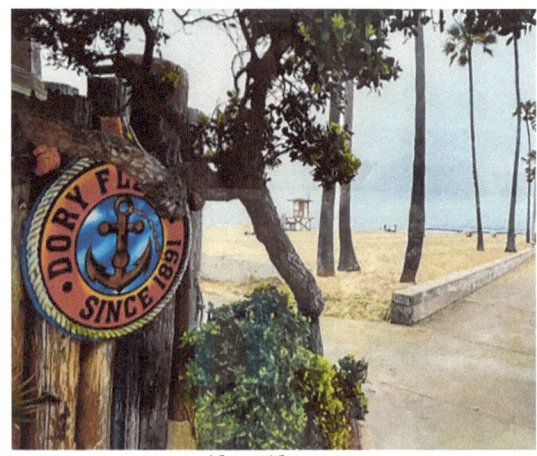
Alex Alarcon

213-373-4361 - www.artsofpoetry.com - artsofpoetry@gmail.com

Corona Art Association

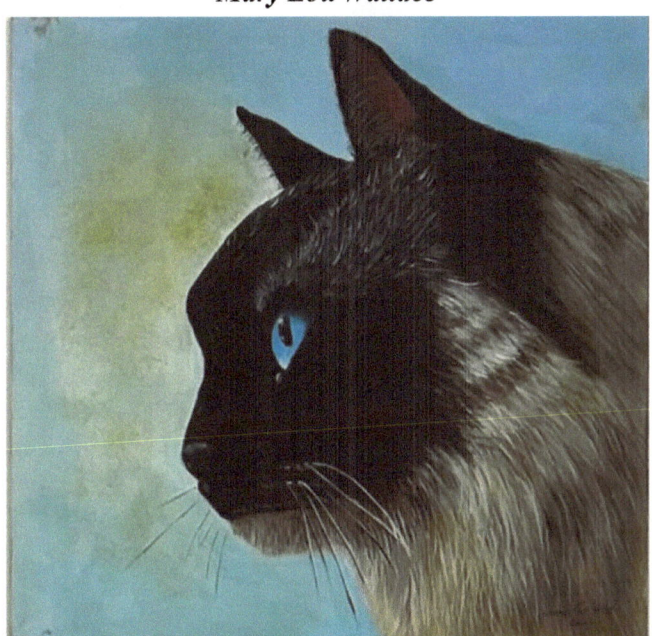
Mary Lou Wallace

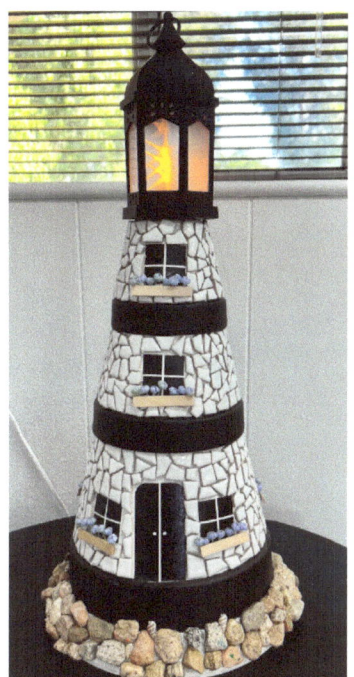
Kim Mabon

They are a 100% volunteer organization and rely on funds generated from art classes, workshops, donations, grants and sales from their new Gallery Shop.

The purpose of the Corona Art Association is to encourage and develop the appreciation, study, and practice of the visual arts and to further educate, inspire and enrich the lives of others.

You will find one-of-a-kind gifts, cards and wearable art, created by local artisans. Shop local and support local artists.

Learn more about the CAA at CoronaArtAssociation.org. Visit the Gallery Shop, Located in the Corona Historic Civic Center. 815 W. Sixth, Street, Suite #145, Corona, CA 92882.

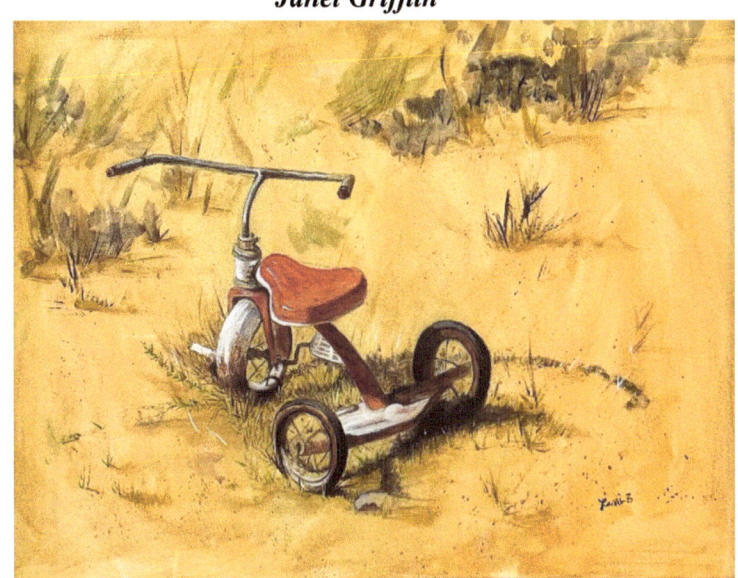
Janet Griffith

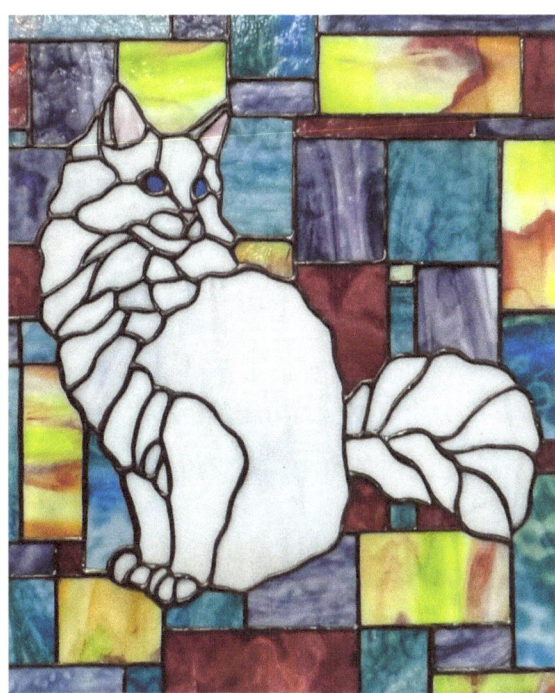
Becky Floyd

213-373-4361 - www.artsofpoetry.com - artsofpoetry@gmail.com

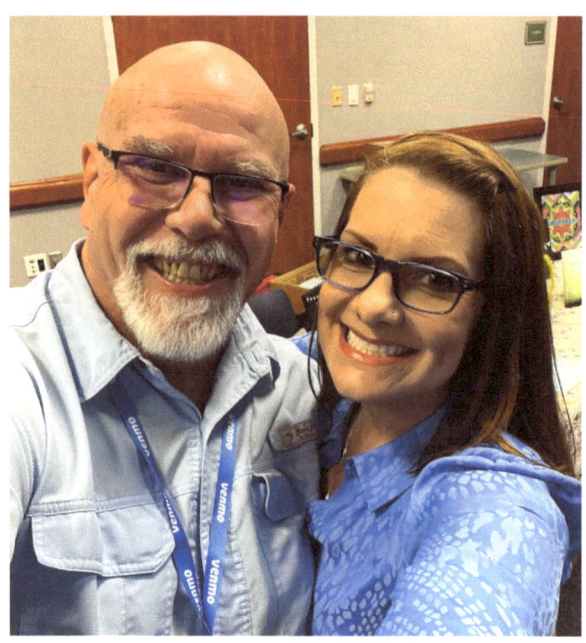

Kevin & Melony Killoren

The universe got together to put two writers together, to show what being together should entail.
We rose above our lessons and we healed, there were mountains to climbs and ships to set sail.
There was a life waiting for us, the timing was right, the universe was setting the table.
We collided through space and time to be a beacon of light, we were ready, willing and able.
We came to shift the vibration of love from all we can see, to beyond what we now can feel.
We joined each other on this journey to show what love is, and how it can be amazing when real.
Keeping It Magical isn't just our business slogan, it's how we live, it's our way of life.
When you truly love someone that doesn't die, it's present through the good and strife.

The failures turn to building blocks, together nothing can stop the magic you share.
It's a total surrender to each other, laying it all on the line laying your naked soul bare.

written by Kevin Killoren

Love Can

We can see how it all makes sense. I can see how it had to be.
We can hear the words our souls cried out. I can hear you calling for me.

We can feel the love that we knew we shared. I can feel your love in every breath.
We know what we had always known. I know that love saved you from death.

We can write the way that lovers can. I can write of this love endlessly.
We can't wait to share this story of love. I can't wait for the whole world to see.

We can't bare another day apart. There's nothing that I wouldn't do.
We can't change their minds but we can win hearts. I can't change the world without you.

written by Melony Killoren

Would you like to be featured in our next issue?

Email your art or poetry to artsofpoetry@gmail.com

Deadline: June 1 2024
ArtsofPoetry.com

213-373-4361 - www.artsofpoetry.com - artsofpoetry@gmail.com

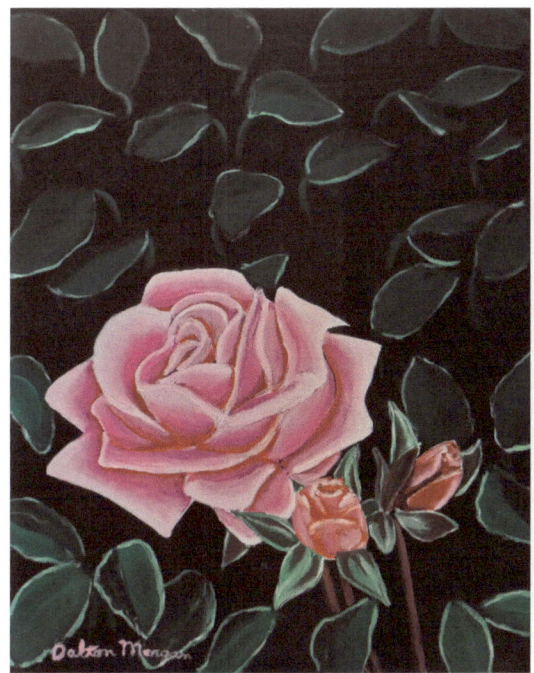
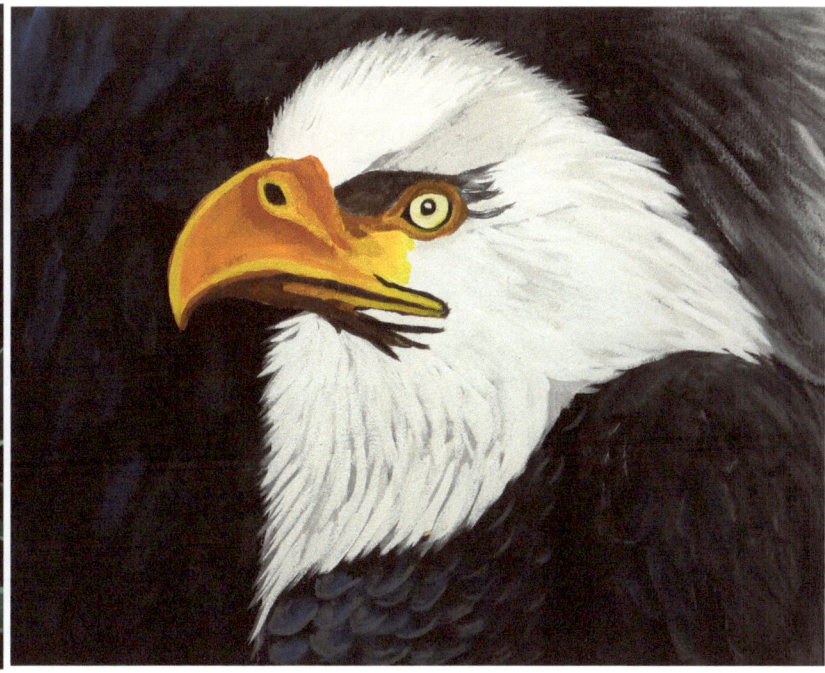
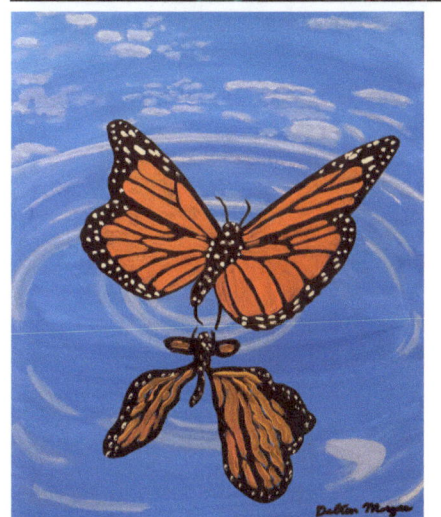

Artist Dalton Alonzo Morgan

Dalton tries to brings life into his paintings. He does a variety of subjects, using acrylics. He also is available to do commission work.
Instagram: daltonalonzomorgan.
On Facebook you will find him as Lonnie Morgan
which is his nickname for Alonzo.
Lonnie is his nickname for Alonzo,
He signs all his paintings as Dalton Morgan
863-242-7682.

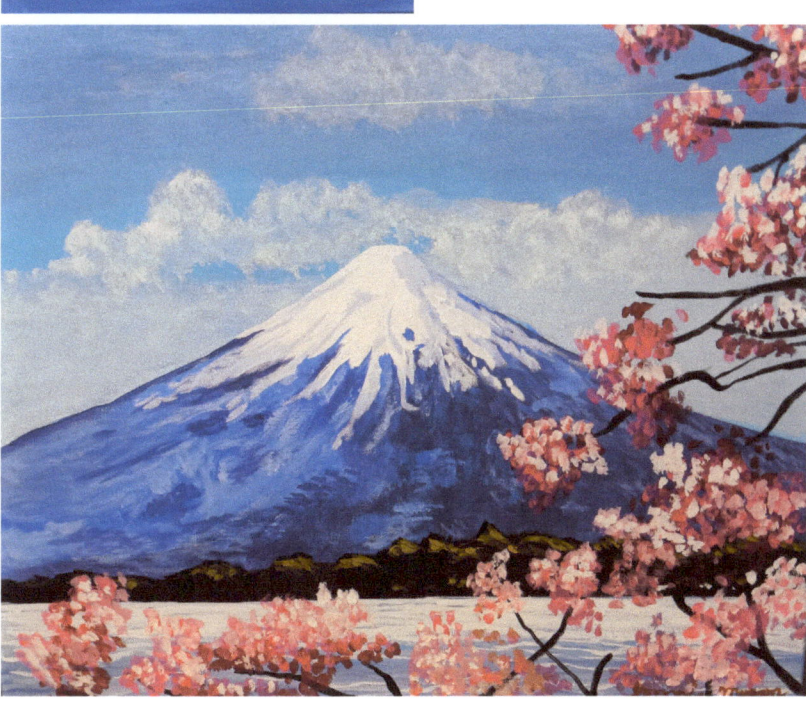
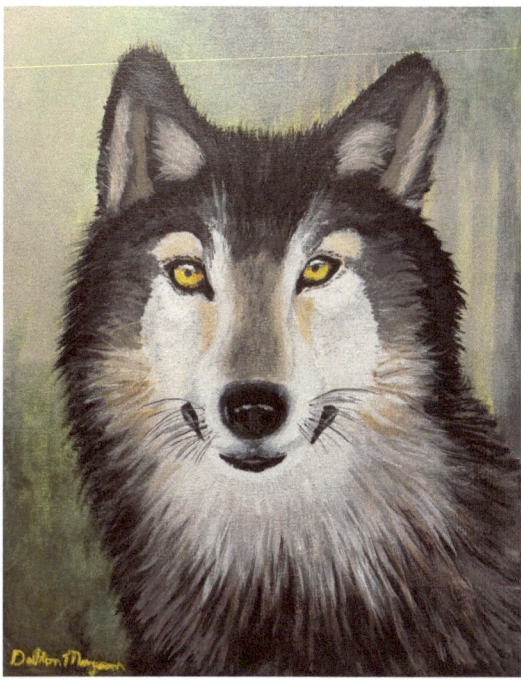

213-373-4361 - www.artsofpoetry.com - artsofpoetry@gmail.com

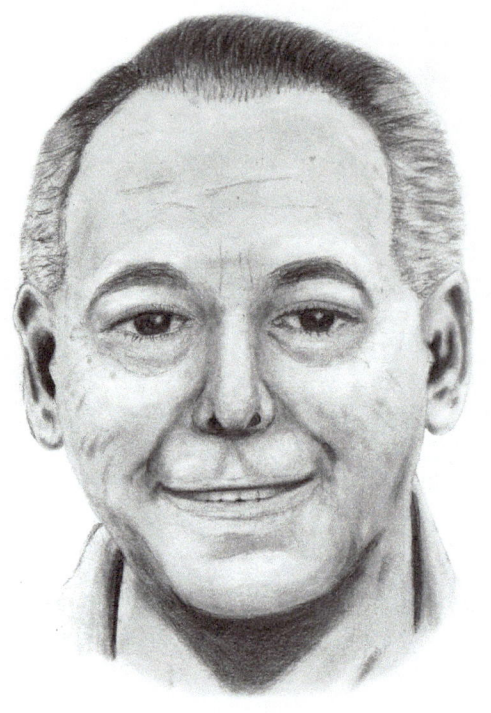
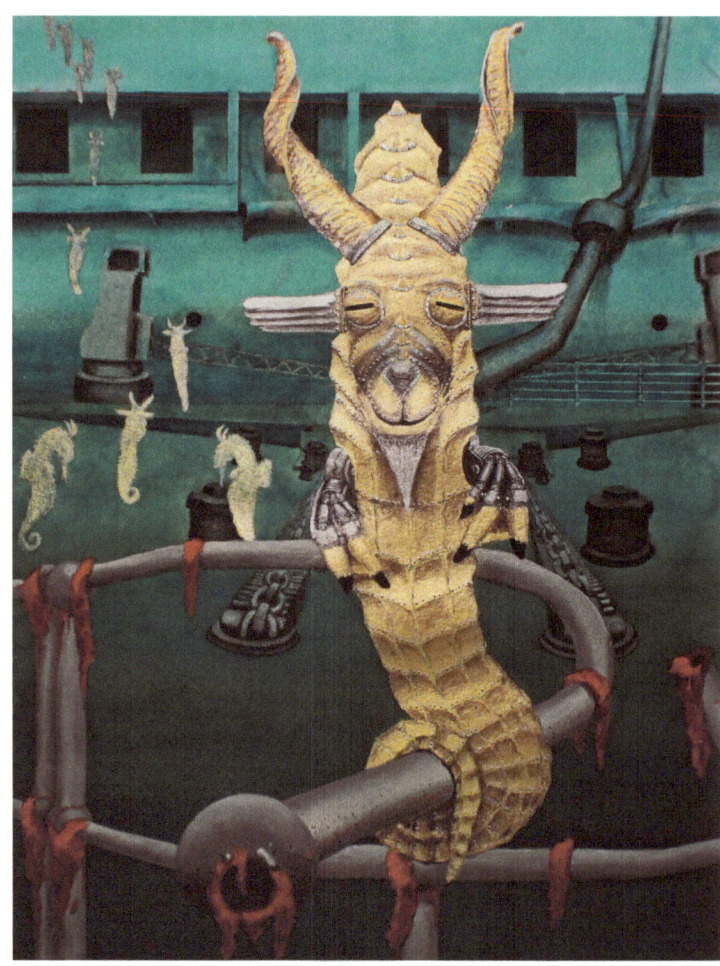

H Benjamin Diaz

As Always Ben has created more master pieces. Absolutely love his SteamPunk Zodiac series. It is the 3 winter Zodiac signs: Capricorn, Sagittarius, and Scorpio.

For more of Ben's spectacular art and collections
https://hbdiazartwall.com

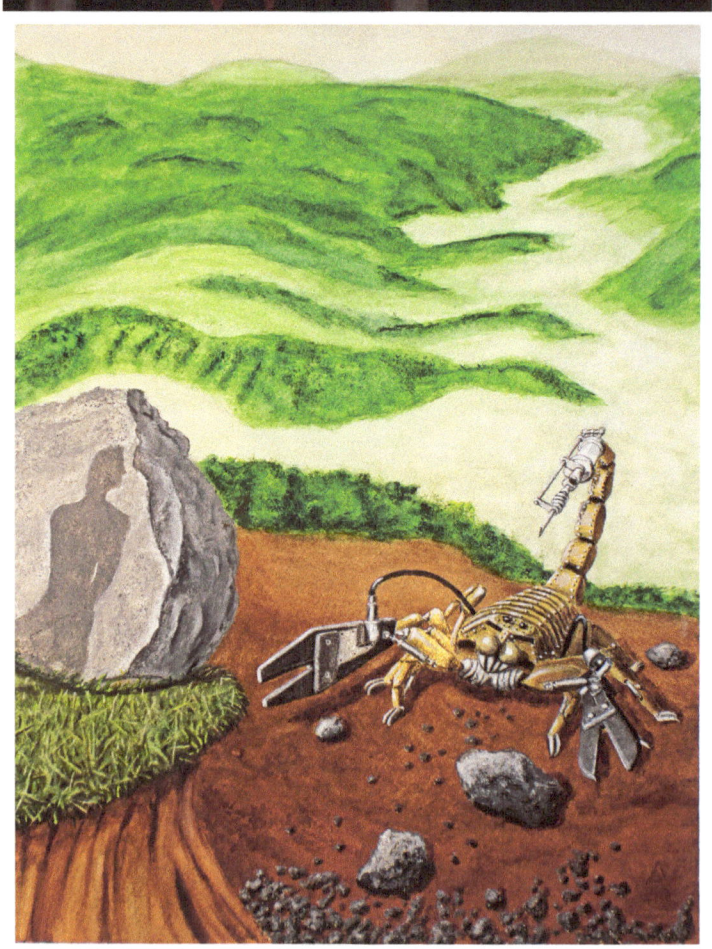

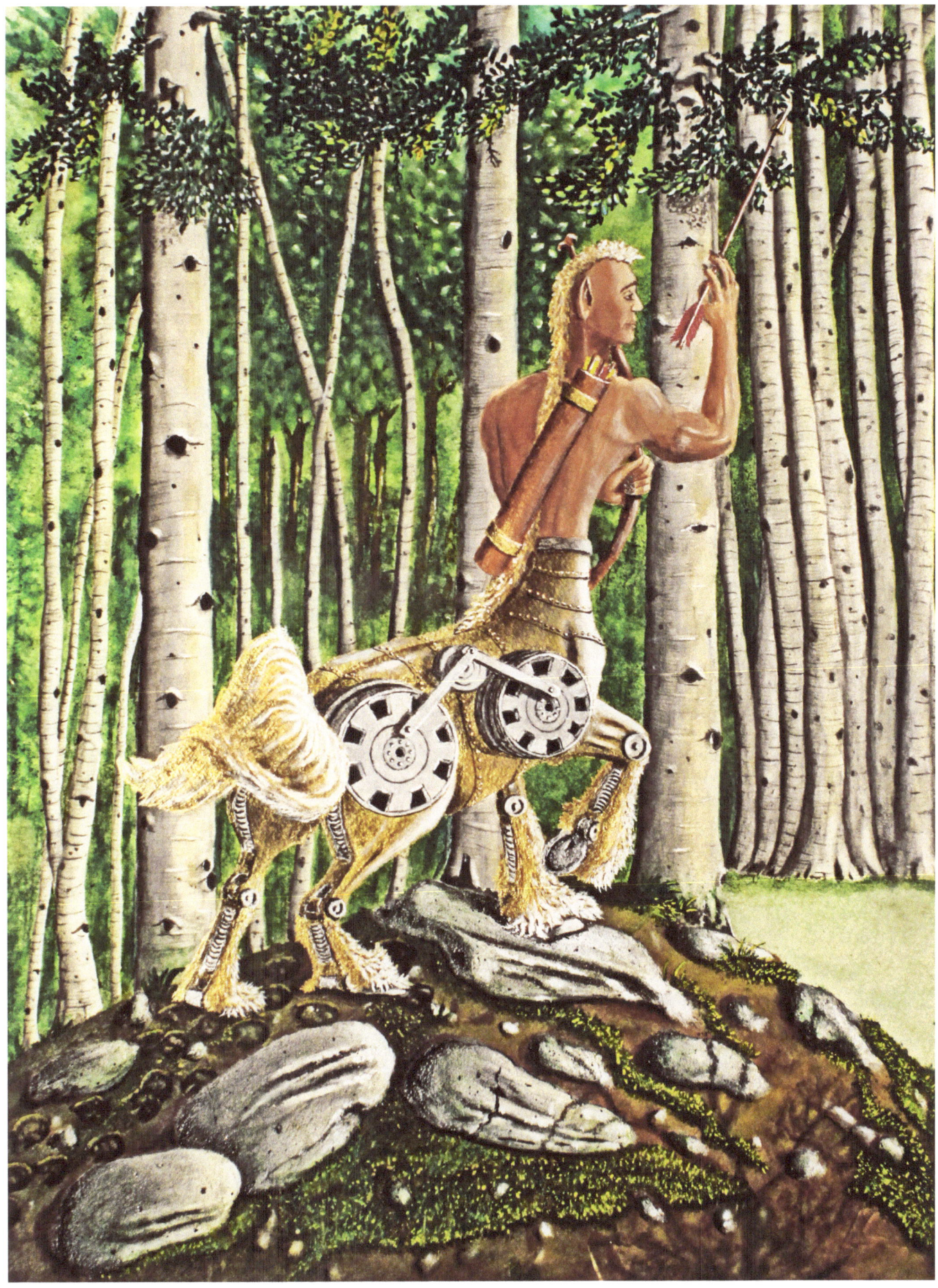

213-373-4361 - www.artsofpoetry.com - artsofpoetry@gmail.com

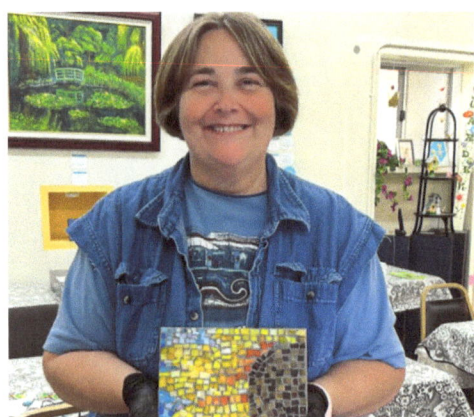

Carol Mae

SWEET COTTAGE HIDEAWAY

Enveloped by sweet grasses, bright blossoms and most cherished antiquities
A beckoning bench sits there awaiting, calling her name
Where her chaotic senses awaken and enlighten
To expand life's small delights
Here time lingers in suspended vignetted moments
Cool breezes, they whisper among emerald leaves
To the woodland fairies' delight
The symphony of birdsong calls out in unison
From sun's first rise until the day's last dim
Here...everyday doldrums are pushed aside
With the flurry of a bee as it passes by
Satin winged butterflies flutter
From soft petal to powdered stamen
Twirling, circling in figure eights
As if dancing in fancy flight
Wings' vibration from hummingbird's journey
Seeking, searching sweetest nectar from trumpet flower
Intricately patterned lizards lie lazily
Helpless upon the warmest stone
Spiders are much more industrious in observation
As they spin their magical, intricately perfect laced webs
To capture their breakfast and twinkling morning dew
Lastly but not least are the slow- going snails
Leaving their glistening trails
To make her take notice
They, too, are a part of this coveted place
A cool place in the grass to wiggle her toes
To touch the dirt, feel the sun upon her cheeks
She revels in the blue sky and fluffed up clouds
Nature's little miracles
Take note of the Master's creation
So much to be appreciated in the alternate world
A space to be and find herself
Only few in number will realize before it's too late
To find their day at one's sweet cottage hideaway
To enjoy a resting place
From the enslaved and hurried
written by Carol Mae
hum_birdz@hotmail.com

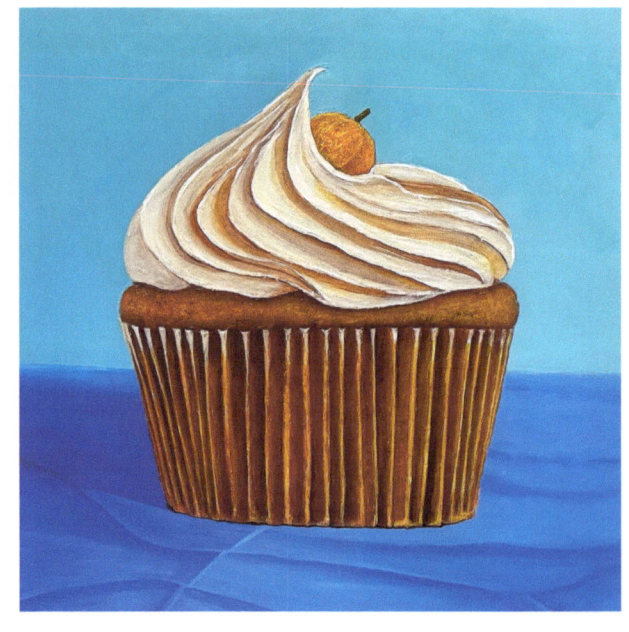

Artist Laureen Pedroza

A sweet taste of heaven in a little cup
filled with sugar and spice as if it's not enough
topped with sweet whipped cream topped with a mini treat
The fullness of it's flavor in one bite it is complete
My tastebuds are melting for this delectable delight
filled with love and care one baked precision is just right
Oh how I love the holidays filled with tastes of every kind
Look and you will discover your sugar passion find.

written by Denise Toro
inspired by Laureen Pedroza cupcake

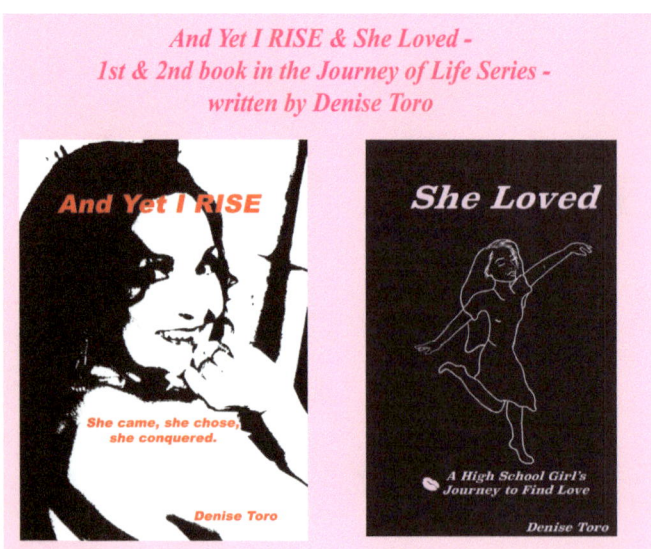

213-373-4361 - www.artsofpoetry.com - artsofpoetry@gmail.com

Artist Keith Slover

For me, drawing and painting is a kind of meditation space where I can get lost in the details of an image as it emerges. I don't know where a picture is going when I start, so its always an intuitive process as I work my way across the page—sort of the story of my life. As an eternal optimist, I'm always looking for the bright side and hoping my process of discovery never ends.

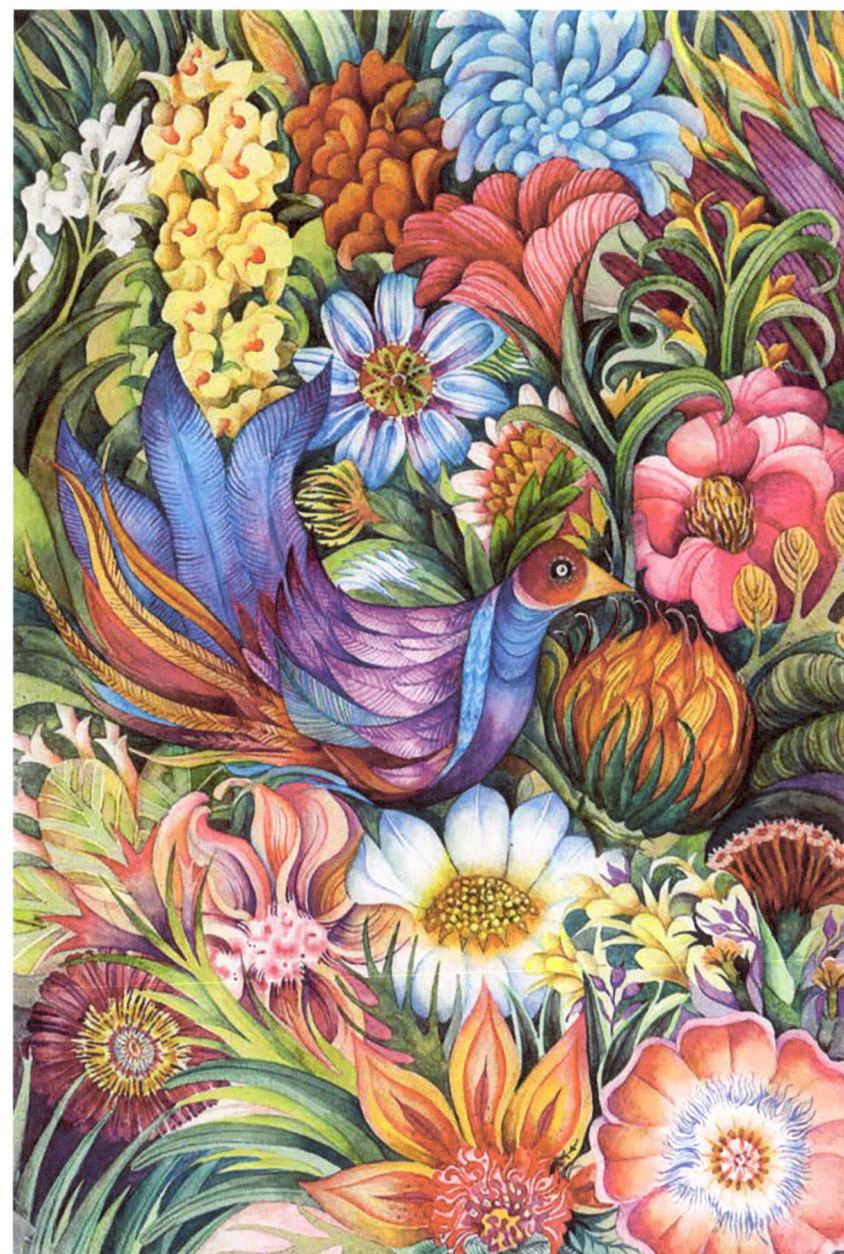

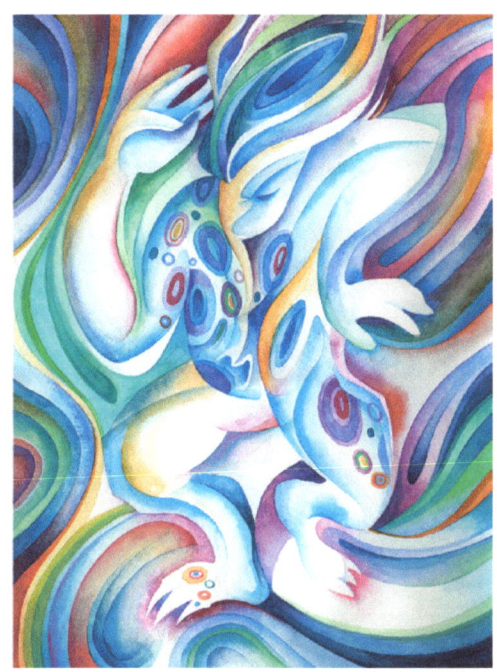

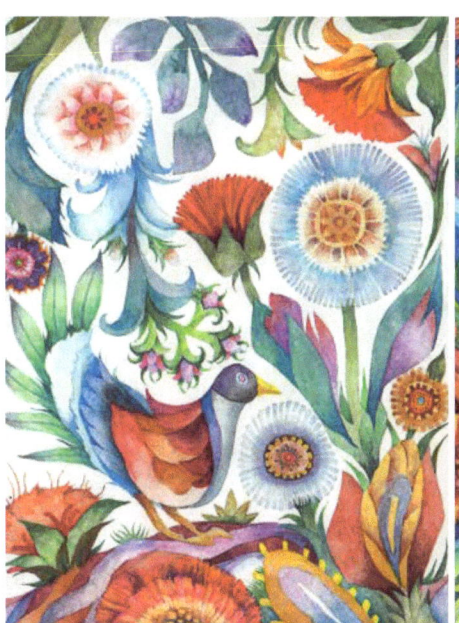

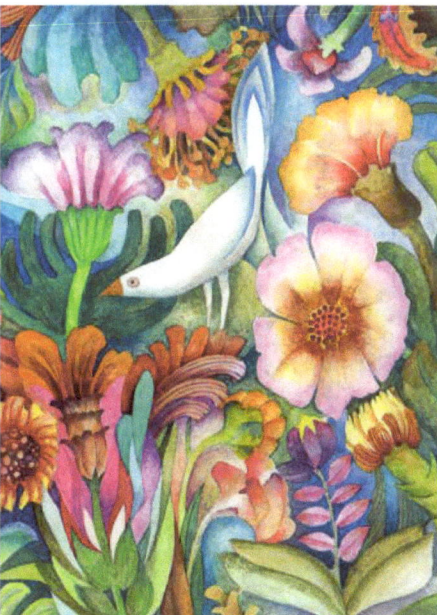

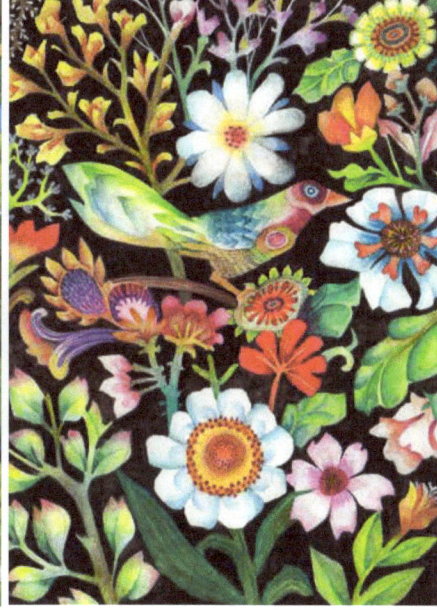

213-373-4361 - www.artsofpoetry.com - artsofpoetry@gmail.com

SQUARE I GALLERY

"Red On Red"

This will be the last artist reception in my Square I Gallery in Claremont
After over 33 years I am moving my Gallery to a new location

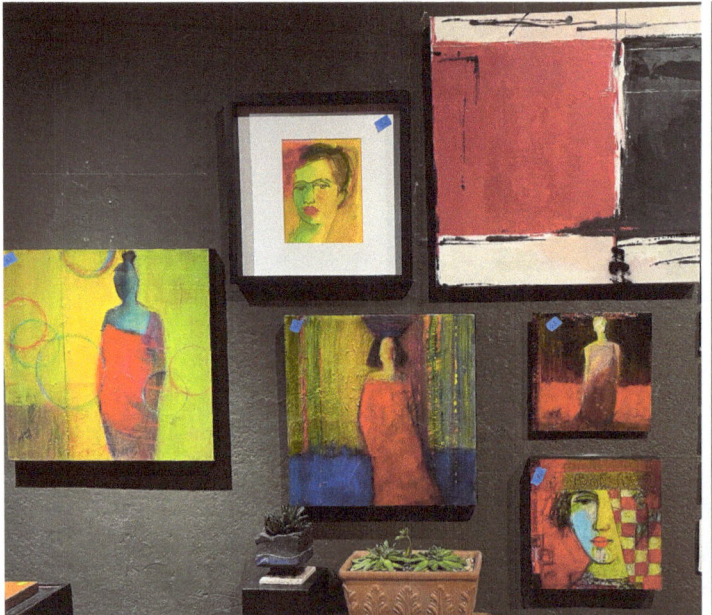
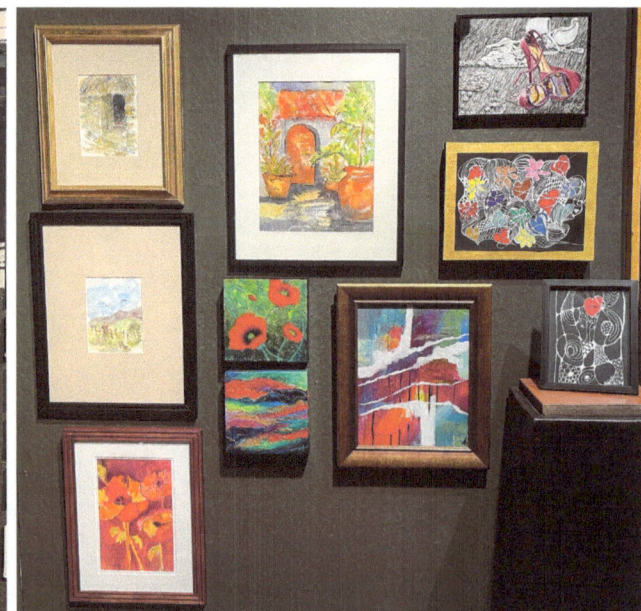

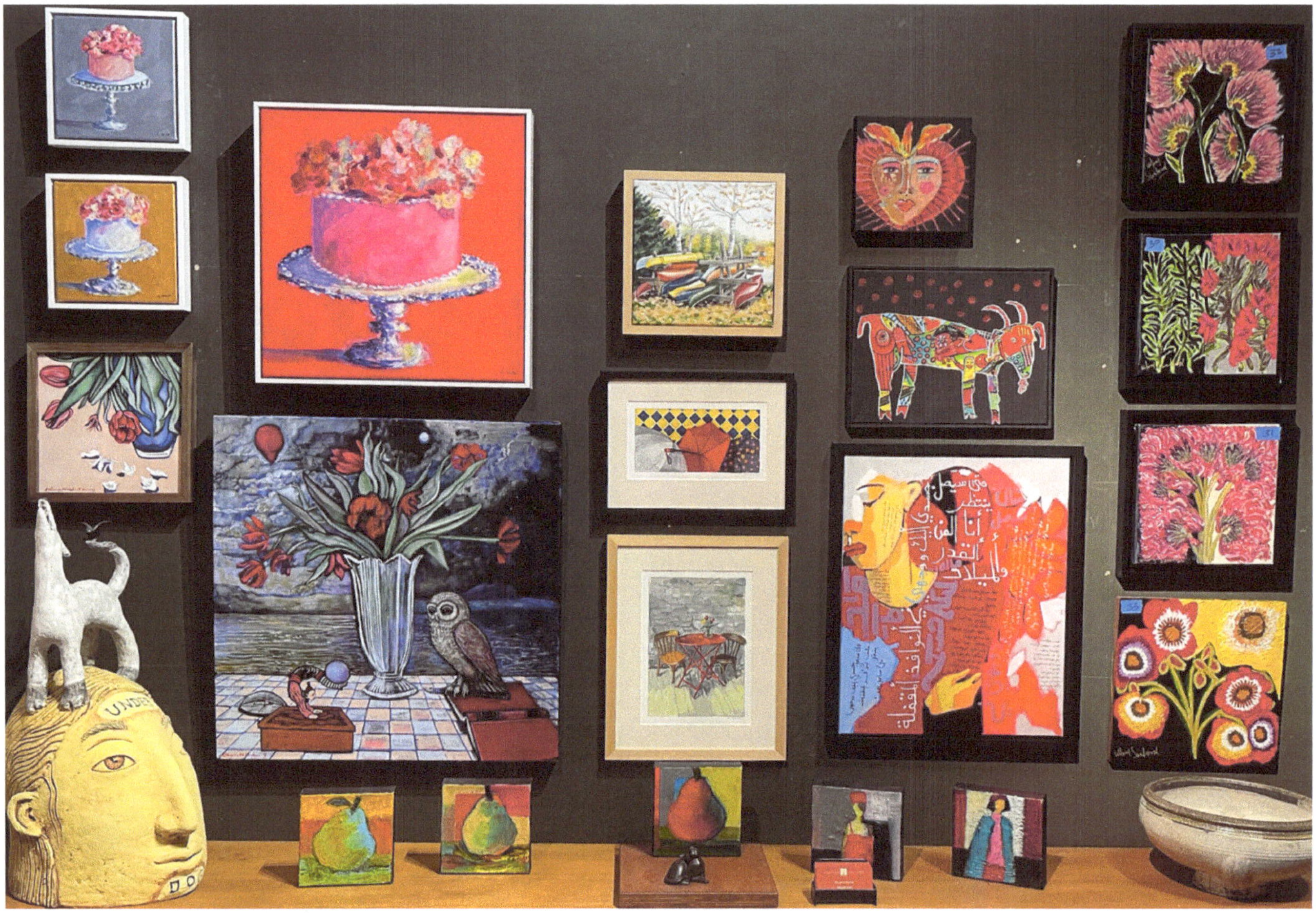

213-373-4361 - www.artsofpoetry.com - artsofpoetry@gmail.com

SQUARE i GALLERY

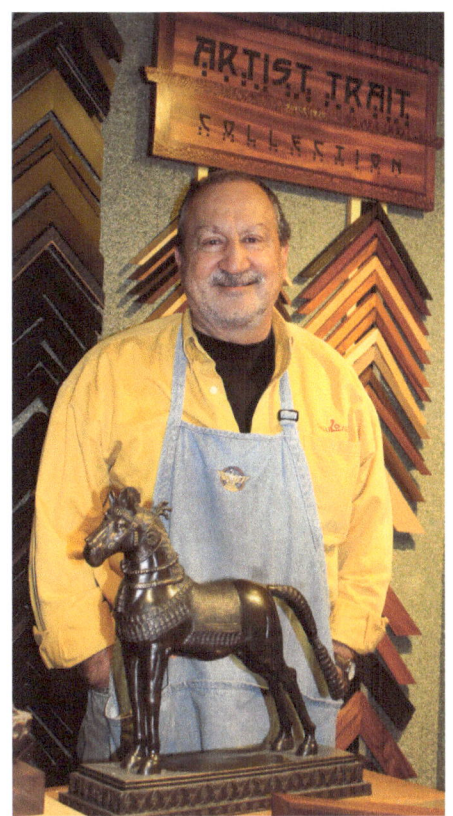

Marodeen Ebrahimzedah

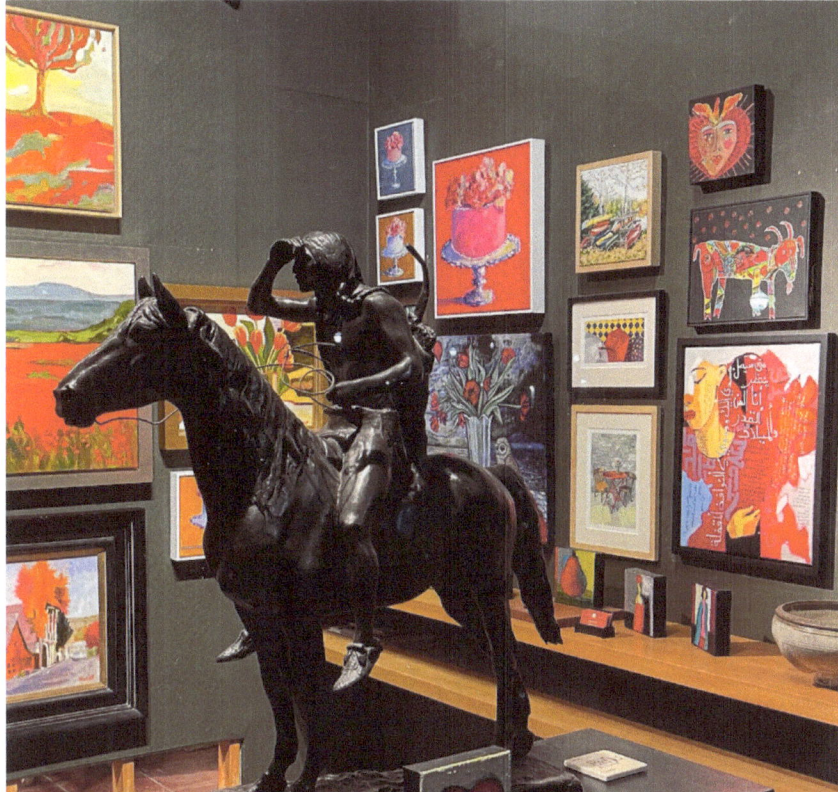

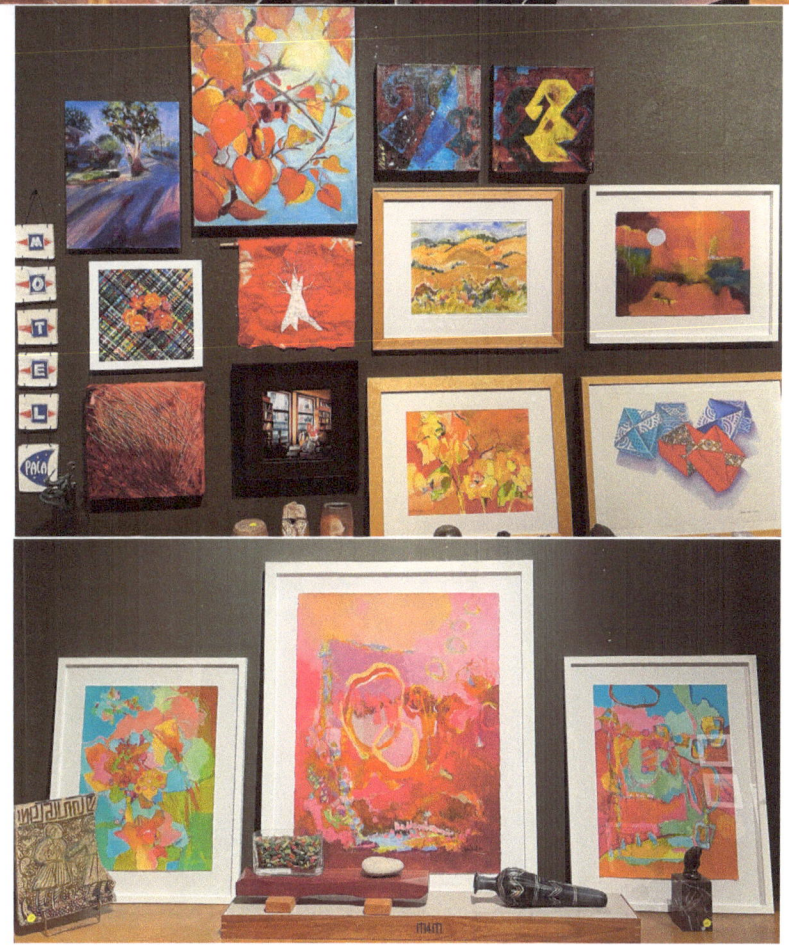

Square i Gallery is an annex to Artist Trait Gallery that was established in 1979 as a fine art gallery with an art services like museum quality customer framing, restoration and appraisal and at the same time coordinating and selling your fine art estate sale.

Square i gallery is a separate division from the Artist Trait solely for exhibiting fine art every month by introducing different artist's work with a reception on the first Friday of each month. This photo album includes some of the memorable moments from some of these shows since 2006

Tues. - Fri. 10 - 1 pm 3 - 6 pm
Saturday 10 - 6 pm
110 Harvard Ave.
Claremont CA 91711
info@squareigallery.com
www.squareigallery.com 909.625.2533

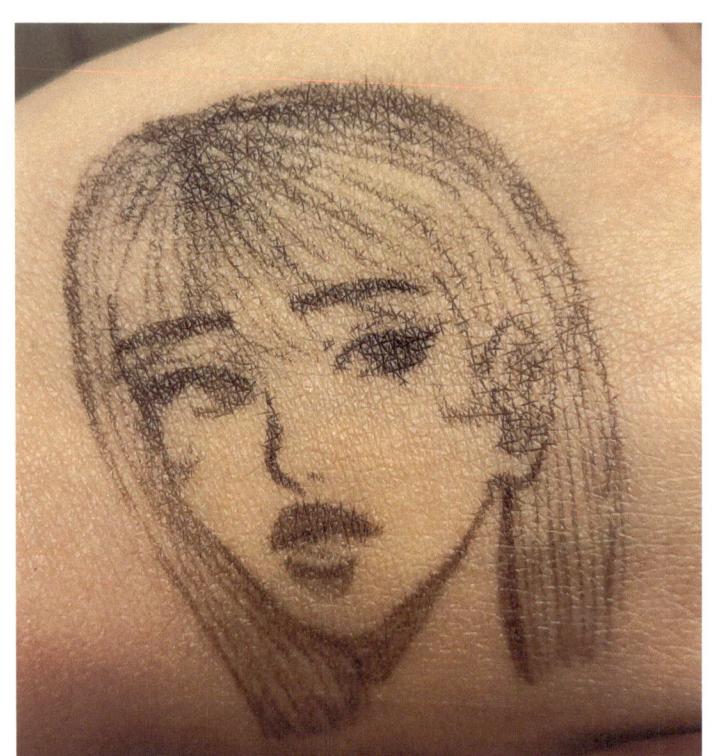
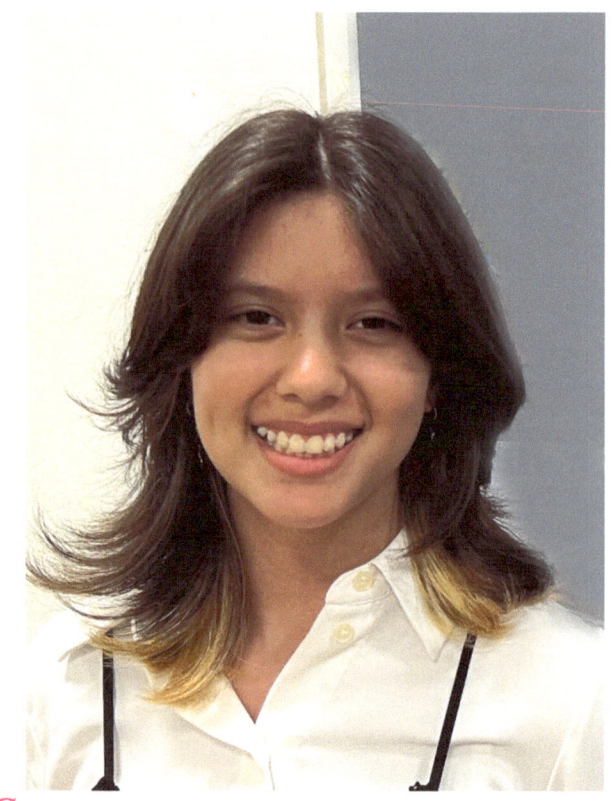

Rachael DeGuzman

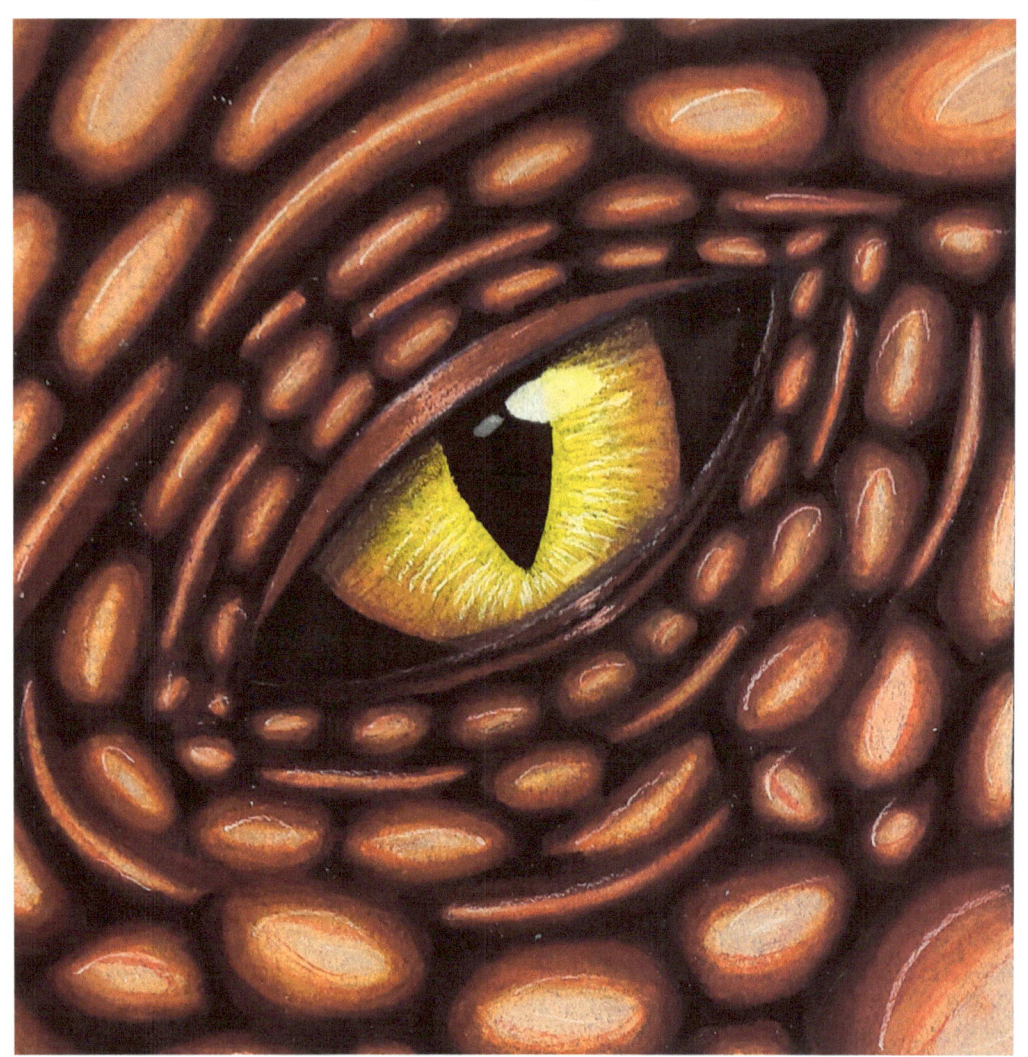

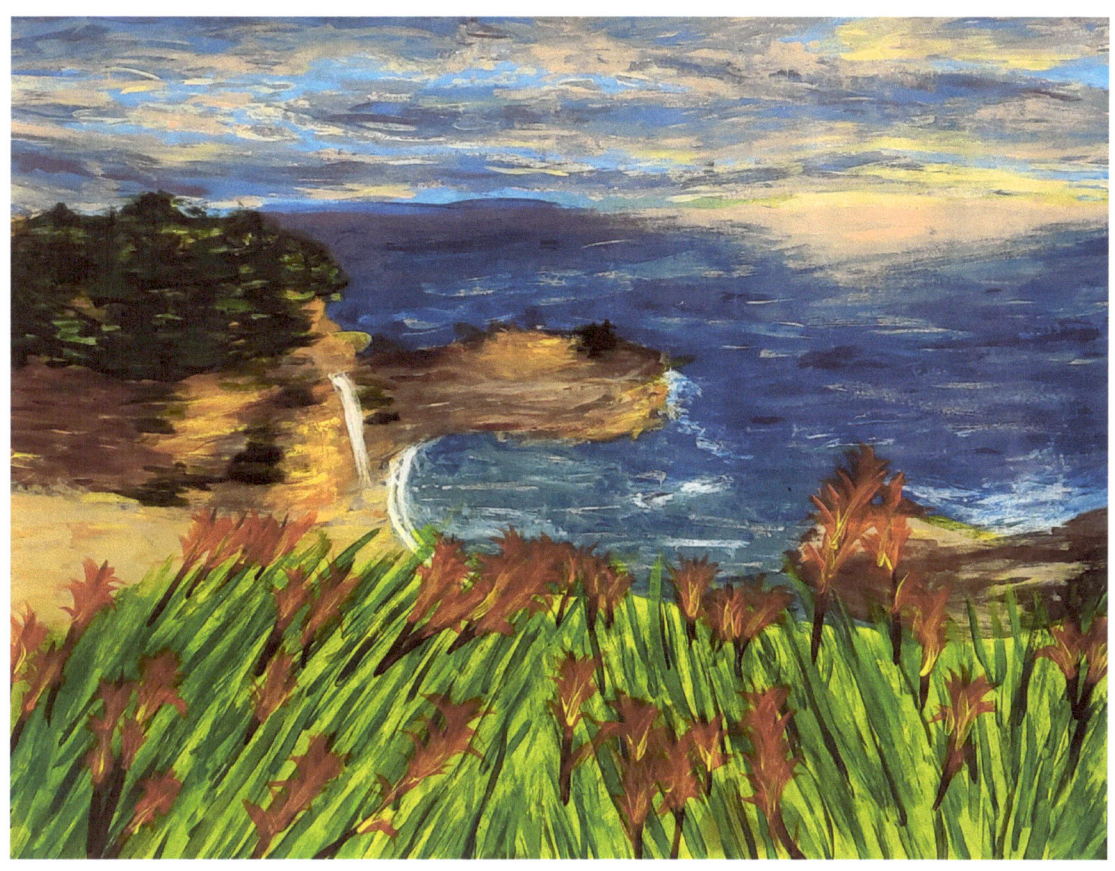

Rachael DeGuzman

I'm 14 years old. I'm a self taught artist. I've loved art ever since I was a kid. I use art as a way to express myself and I hope to pursue art as a profession in the future. Art has become an important part of my life and now everything around me inspires me, from people to scenery, and even music.

Rachael's art piece to the right won Clifton Middle School's, second place in MAFA (Monrovia Association of Fine Art) as student artist competition.

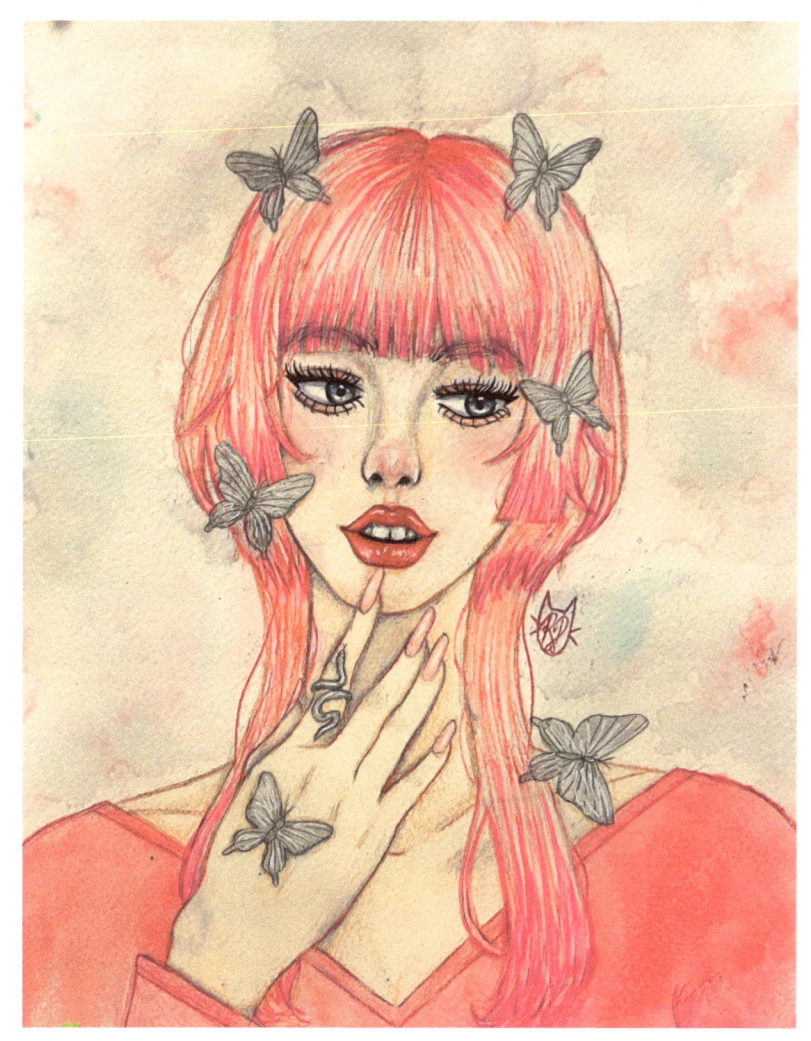

213-373-4361 - www.artsofpoetry.com - artsofpoetry@gmail.com

Author DrBendetta Perry
SPOKEN WORD

At the age of 18. I became a Spoken Word Artist!!!
Read Psalm 91

God has called us all to speak the Word of God over our lives with Authority releasing his power and Anointing to cancel the enemies assignment to destroy us. For once the Word is spoken it releases angels assigned to our lives to go forth and assist those who are heirs of salvation according to Hebrews 1:14. To each believer for our lives and destiny to reach for his glory. The spirit of the Lord came to me at age 18 in a dream and told me to read aloud Psalm 91. Immediately, before going to school, I read the whole chapter Psalm 91 aloud which released my angels to combat the enemy on my behalf. The same day in the evening around 9pm. I was leaving a youth service and on my way home, I stopped at the corner store to buy a can of soda. Left the store and attempted to cross a major street with no cross a major street with no crosswalk or traffic light. I stepped off the curb and I heard a voice of the angel assigned to my life say: "Step back you left your bible on the counter of the store. Instantly, I took one step back without turning around, and there came a car speeding so fast, that if I had not stepped back the impact of the speeding car would have left me badly wounded or dead.

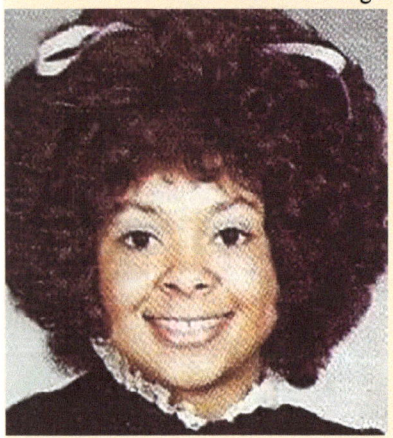

Reading Psalm 91 aloud saved my life at 18 to fulfill the call of God over my life to bring souls to the Kingdom of God and I became a teenage Evangelist throughout my community and high school.

Wisdom Key: Become a Spoken Word Artist by speaking God's Word over your life daily and watch God move on your behalf. Author DrBendetta Perry, Day 8 of my book "Uplifting Encouragement for the Soul 31 Day Journey to the Promises of God."

Fragrance of the Spirit God's Aroma Ministry
fragrancesofthespirit.com

It's a Gift

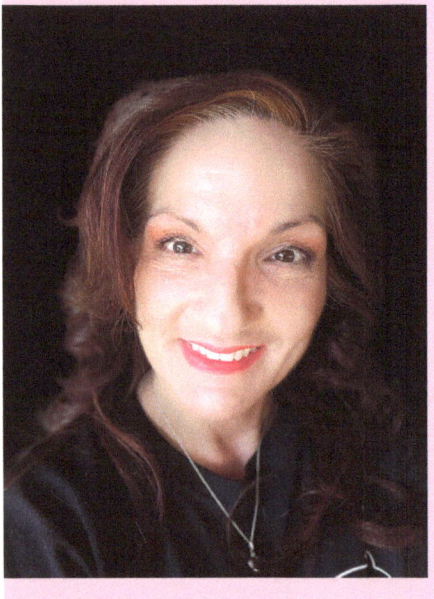

Denise Toro

It's a gift you know,
The reason why we write,
It's thoughts and dreams that come to life,
It's our prayers, emotions, deep within our soul,
Seeking to find the answers unroll,
It's our eyes sweet pictures on paper displayed,
Of Life of dreams of yesterday,
Somewhere in our hearts lies the keys to our hopes,
Wishing to seek what no one else knows,
As the pen touches paper and the artist emerge,
Let's go of the ink as the energy will surge,
Through an atmospheric electrical pulse in our hearts,
Comes the stories we write where the world becomes part.

Written by Denise Toro

213-373-4361 - www.artsofpoetry.com - artsofpoetry@gmail.com

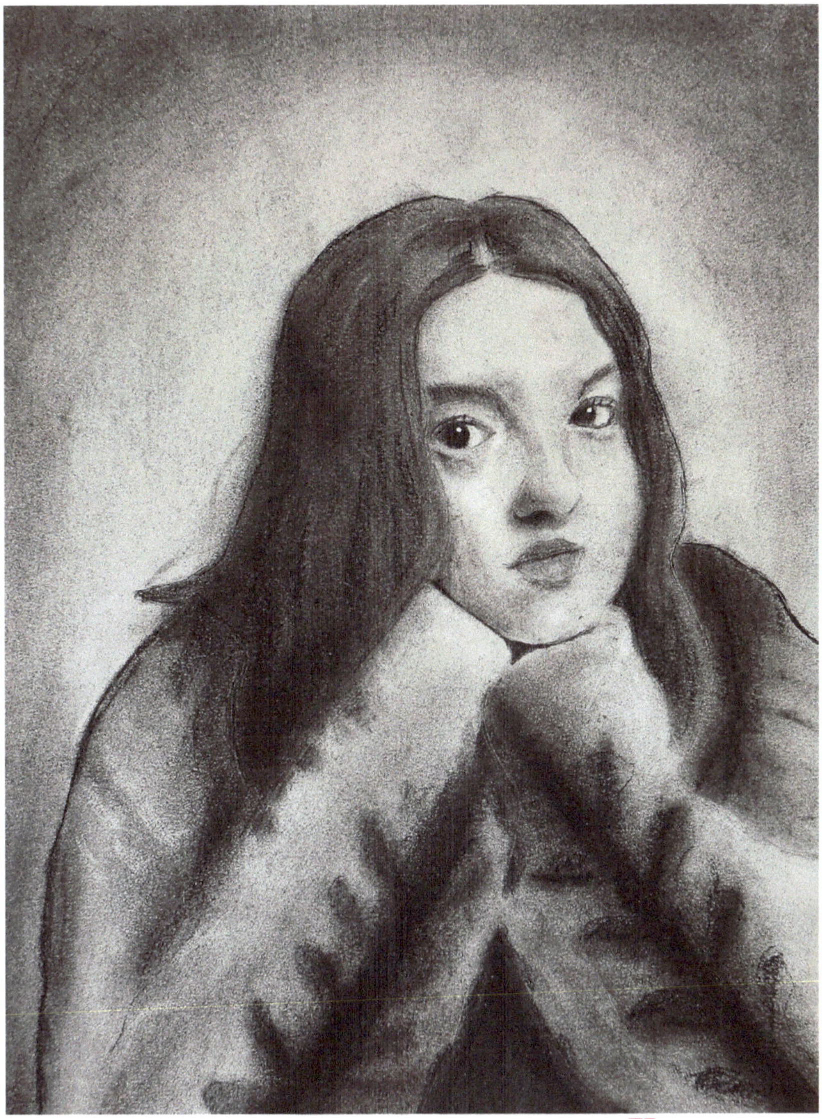

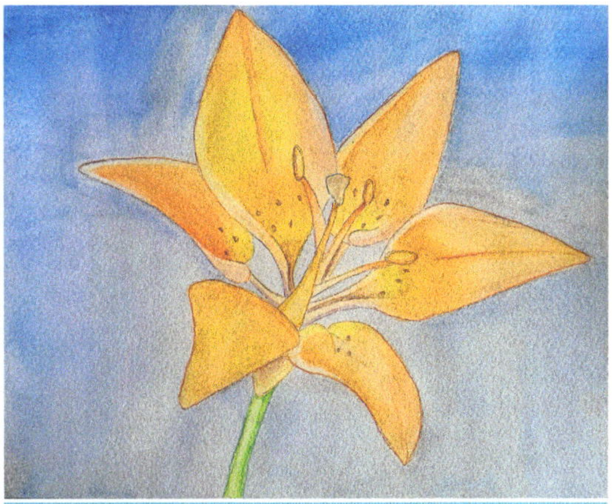

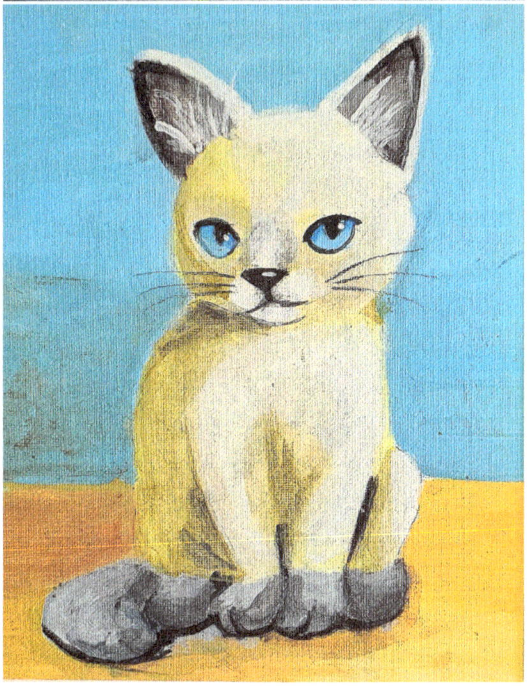

Kaavya

I'm a fifteen year old that loves to read, write, and draw. I'm a creative person who loves creating and consuming all forms of art. In my free time, I love taking my dog on walks, listening to music, and baking.

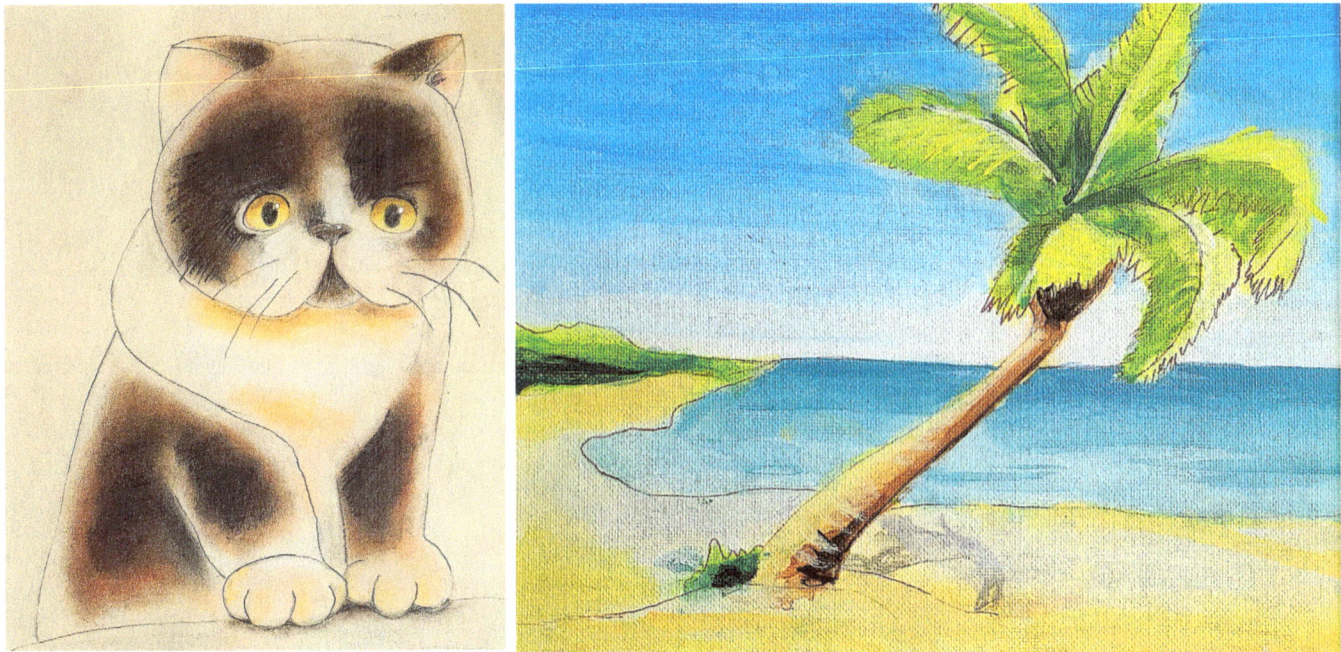

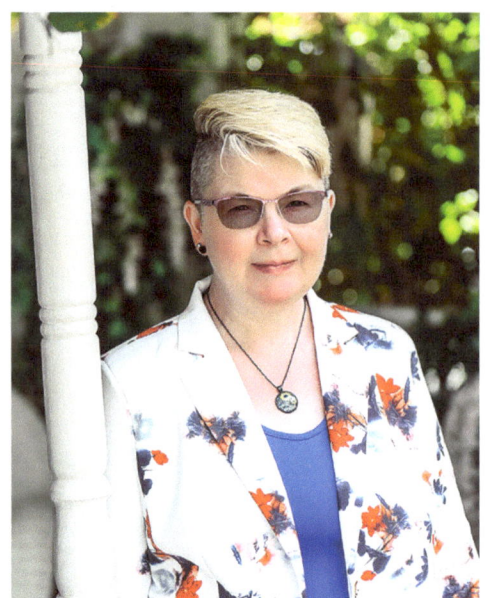

Alicia Wyneken

Blue Balloon
Inspired by Nada Fakhreddine's "The Party is Over"

a red balloon
within a blue balloon
over a dozen like the donuts
set on the table for guests

a blue timescape
underneath a shoe
after the yellow skirt
hops on each balloon
as if playing a child's game

what's left behind
on the ground
the balloon deflated
a print after it pops:
shadows sprinkle on the ground

ah – a breath

a red balloon
hidden under the black shoes

Who is playing hopscotch?

written by Alicia Wyneken, M.S, M.F.A

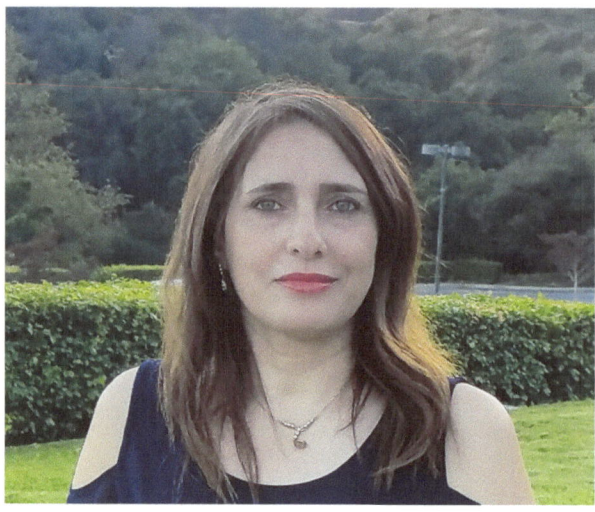

Nada Fakhreddine

"Blue Balloon" is an example of some of the collaborative work the two artists have begun. Nada and Alicia have been collaborating since they met at Claremont Graduate University in 2022, and several of their pieces were featured during CGU's Spring Art Showcase. Nada and Alicia's friendship is joined by culture and belonging to the Mediterranean Sea, where they grew up

Nada Fakhreddine is a visual artist. She works primarily in acrylic, charcoal, and graphite. In her art, she recreates specific, mundane moments of her life. Capturing the charm of such ordinary moments by making visible otherwise invisible aspects of the experience. Nada holds a master's degree in art from Claremont Graduate University. Her art has been featured in the Foothill Poetry Journal. Nada has exhibited her work in both solo and group shows in Southern California.

Alicia Wyneken is a scholar, writer, and educator. She is currently living in California. She has a Bachelor's degree in English from the University of Alaska, Fairbanks, a Master's in Fine Arts, Creative Writing Poetry, and Literature from Antioch University, Los Angeles, and a Master's of Science in Psychology from Mount Saint Mary's University, Los Angeles. She is currently a Ph.D. student in Cultural Studies at Claremont Graduate University, Claremont. Alicia is also a consultant for the Foster Kinship program at Antelope Valley College, Palmdale.

Alicia is an advocate for Diversity, Equity, and Inclusion. She adopted four children from the foster care system and is dedicated to advocating for their needs and other foster care children. She grew up in Nice, France, and has family ties to Martinique. Her research, writing, and heart are connected to both landscapes. Alicia's creative work, essays, and poetry have been published in several small presses and anthologies online and in print in the US and the UK.

Artist Nada Fakhreddine

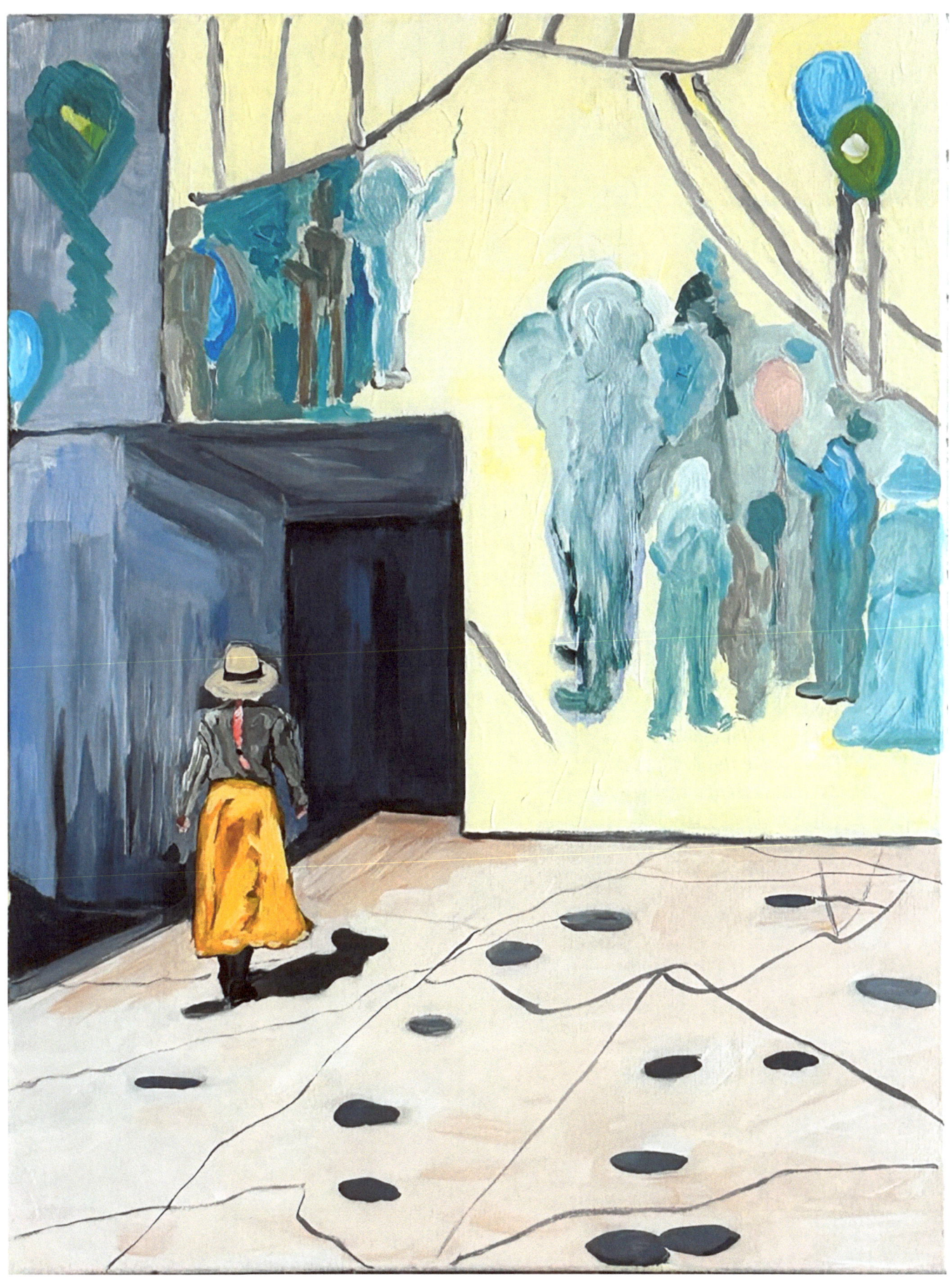

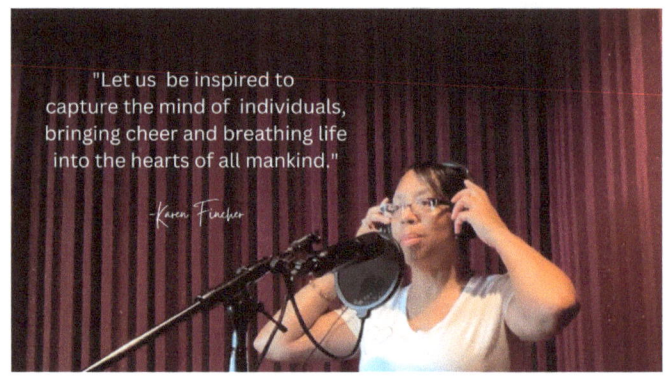

Poet Karen Fincher

Amazing

*Love follows the winding roads
Through the twists and turns
To yield the cold.
Love twinkles as midnight fades,
So you can easily find your way.
It's so amazing to rise with the sun
Yet easily forgotten
Once the day is done.*

You Will Find Me

*You will find me
Amongst the scattered faces,
Feathered by the absence of light.
Between the heavens …
Past the forest of muted green,
Buried within the treasures
Lost in the surge of a storm,
And in the midst of a crowded room,
Standing next to you.
You Will Find Me,
You Will Find Me.*

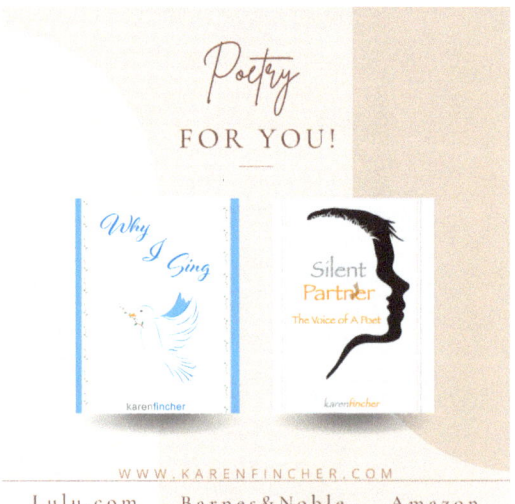

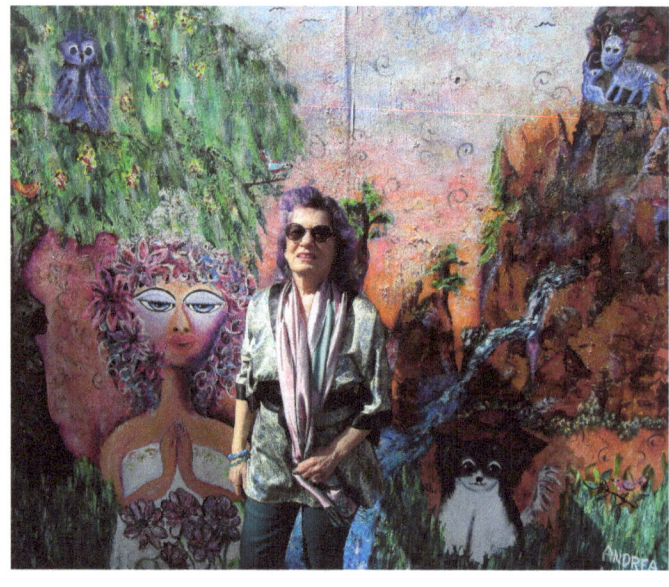

Andrea Willow

Art has been a part of my life for many years. I am an abstract expressionist artist. I paint intuitively and listen to the whispers of my heart and soul. I never know what will emerge. The challenge of my evolving art is to see each piece emerge to completion. I love using colors and textures to create original and exciting art. My intention is to offer a visual piece for the viewer to pause, reflect and stretch their imagination. See if you can match the following titles to each photo. "Buddha Belly Mountain," "Flower Goddess," "Life is a Circus," "Angel of Peace," and "Pray for All". Enjoy! I may be reached at picassotp219@gmail.com.

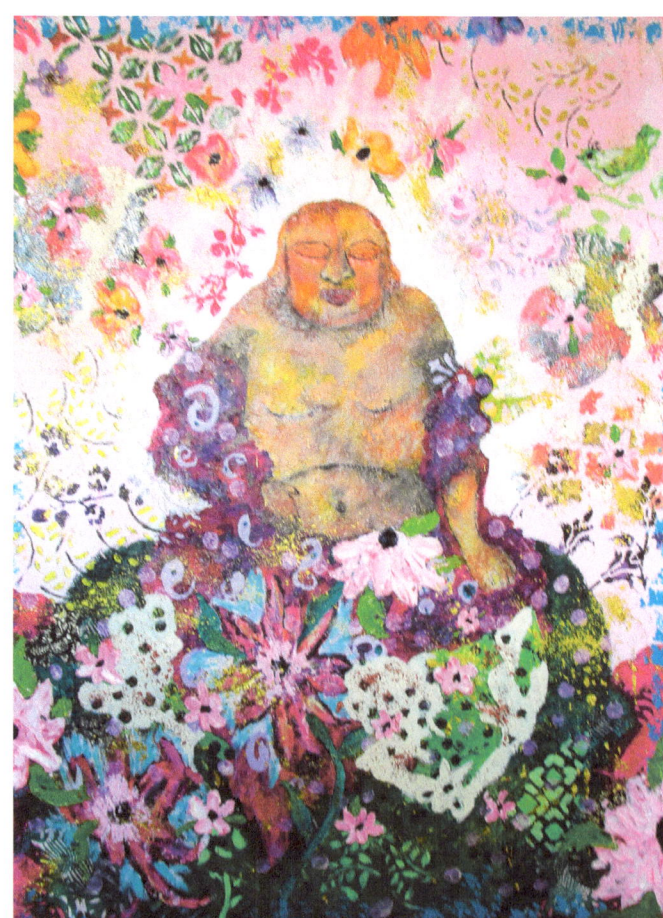

213-373-4361 - www.artsofpoetry.com - artsofpoetry@gmail.com

Artist Andrea Willow

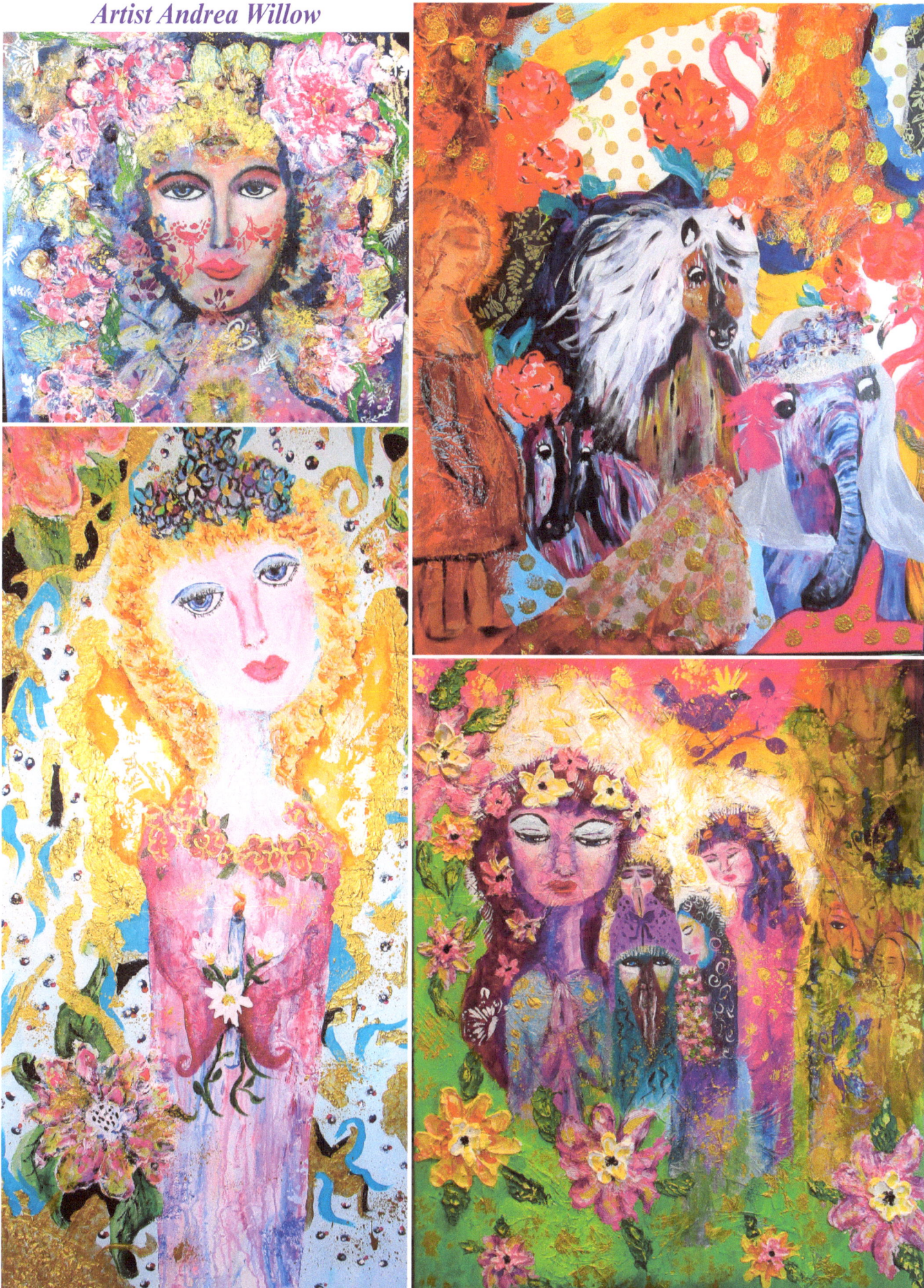

213-373-4361 - www.artsofpoetry.com - artsofpoetry@gmail.com

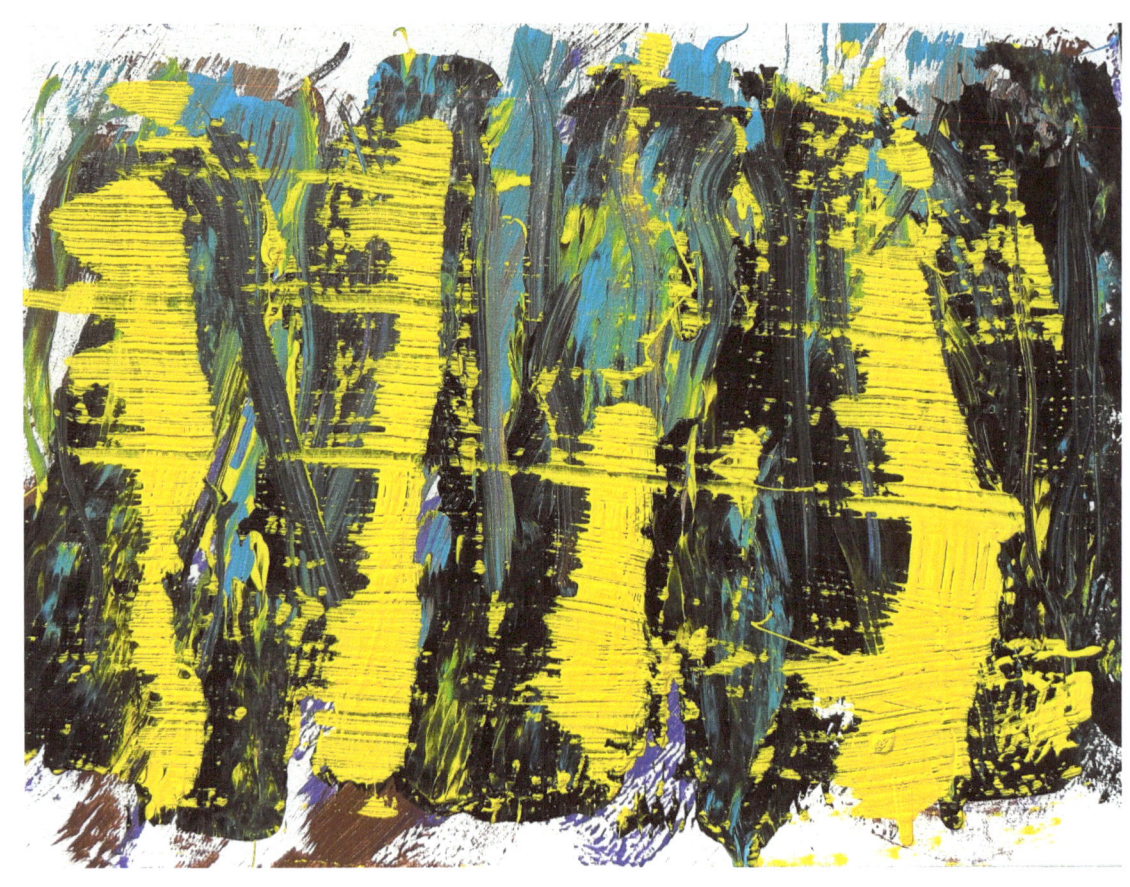

Artist & Poet - Marc Shapiro

ART…WHY?

Art
This is why we do it
To be loved
To be hated
To get laid
To make big bucks
To make big noise
And get away with it
To justify insanity
To justify not working hard
To piss off our parents
And finally
Art
We do it
Because we must

Poetry and Art by

MARC SHAPIRO
AUTHORMARCSHAPIRO@HOTMAIL.COM

By day I am an author of nearly 100 celebrity biographies including, most recently, Keanu Reeves Excellent Adventure and Bukowski On Film. I am also the author of a book of poetry entitled Existential Jibber Jabber as well as a number of short stories and assorted poems that have appeared in publications nationally and internationally. I actually make a living doing this. Don't tell the authorities.

It is only in the last five years that I started painting, first as a way to break the tension of the everyday writer's life and, in the past year, as an abstract outlet for artistic chance and coincidence. I have no formal artistic training. I pride myself on the fact that no two paintings are exactly alike. When I set down to paint, it is all of the moment. Art is Art. This is how I take my artistic walk.

Marc Shapiro is a juried member of the Monrovia Association Of Fine Arts and has exhibited his works this summer on the annual Monrovia Art Walks.
 authormarcshapiro@ yahoo.com

Artist PSW Pamela Wagstaff

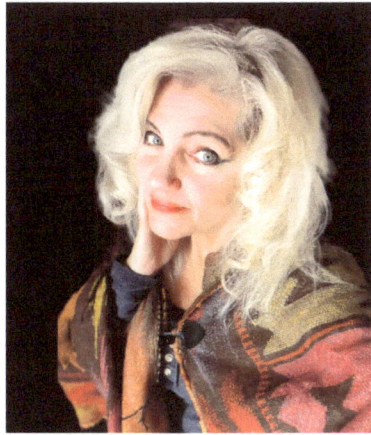

Instagram - ArtByPSW
artistpsw@gmail.com
Art & Poetry Books by PS Wagstaff
amazon.com/author/pswagstaff
www.barnesandnoble.com/s/Pswagstaff

Pamela beautiful piece to the left is inspired by: The story of the Samaritan woman, at the well in the Bible.

Picture bottom right: The inspiration is a Spanish girl. They wore flowers in their hair while dance dancing. As I watched the Ramona outdoor play, pageant in Hemet. The theme was a Spanish girl in love with a Native American Man.

Picture bottom left: It's to reveal ones true self. To be authentic or to process true real beauty

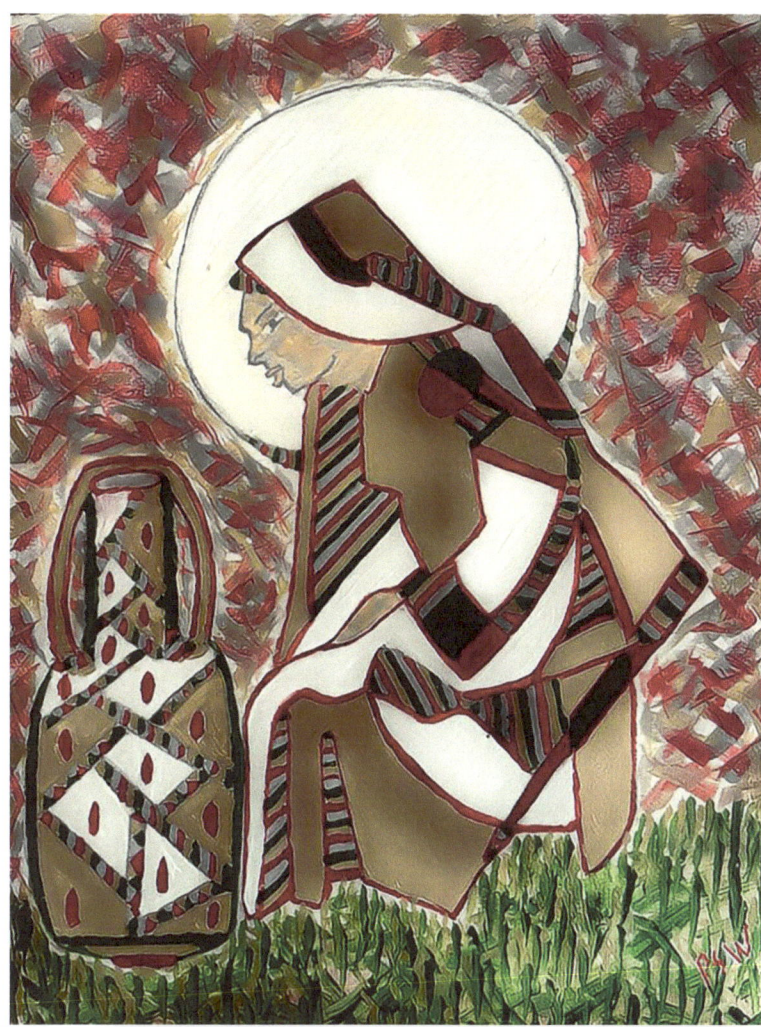

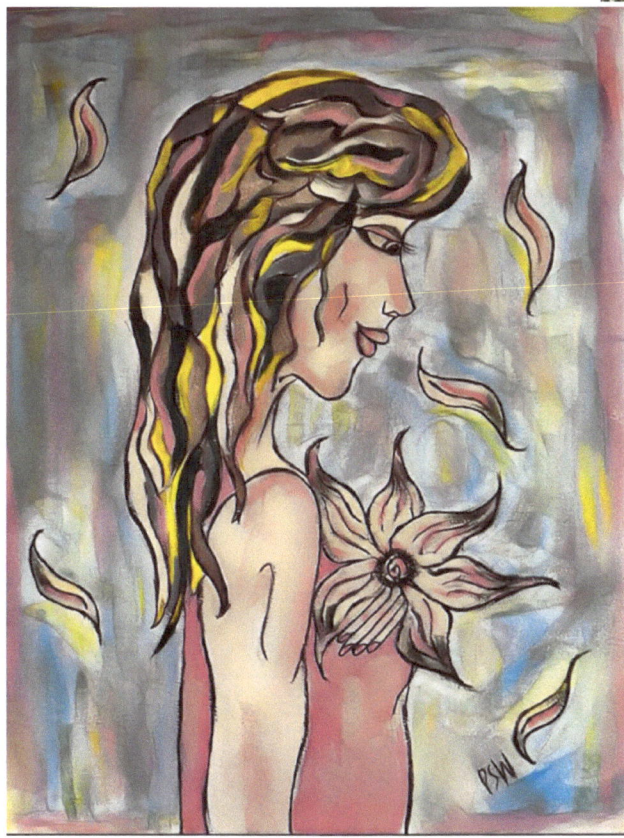

Unfolding

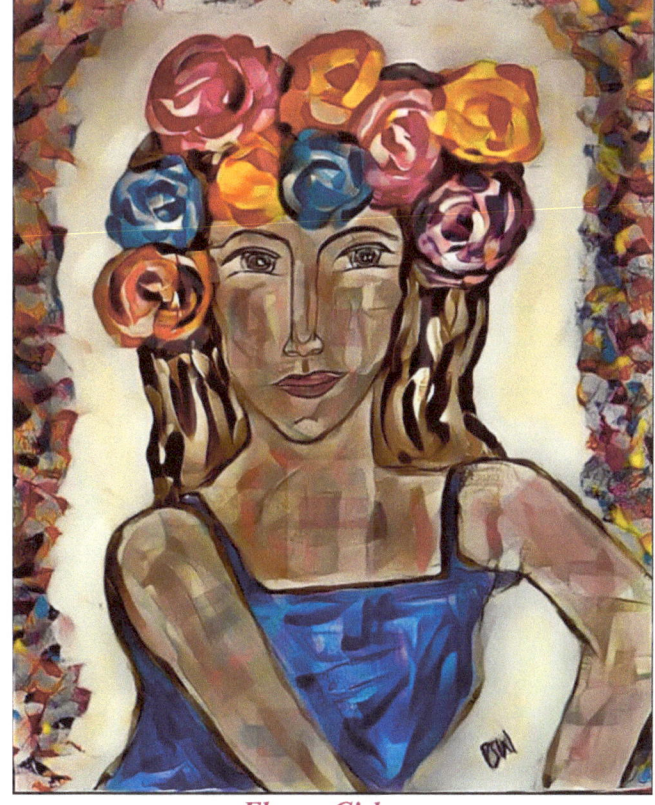

Flower Girl

213-373-4361 - www.artsofpoetry.com - artsofpoetry@gmail.com

Ginger Lai - Sacred Geometry

'Art is about uplifting people. About making them happy. Art is about what is best in the world.'-- *Ginger Lai*

About 7 months ago, I began, purely by happenstance, a psychological and spiritual transformation that has had a profound effect on my life and my art. Though I have been meditating daily since the age of 10, the new experience of a weekly sound bath and increasing my mediation to 2 ½ hours a day has afforded me a new perspective on my art. This has led to a transformation in my artwork - from the abstract to the more ordered vision of the Sacred Geometry that permeates the world around us. Sacred Geometry is the study of the spiritual nature and meaning of the shapes, forms and patterns in the surrounding natural world. This Sacred Geometry, I believe, is also evident in the circle of life itself, from birth to death, in the process of aging, the accumulation of wisdom, and even in the possibility of other selves across a multiverse of possibilities. The repeating patterns of my work can be viewed not only in each individual work of art or piece of jewelry, but as parts of a greater whole, each work relating to those that came before and those to come after and I have committed to creating 100 pieces of Sacred Geometry in a variety of mediums and formats.

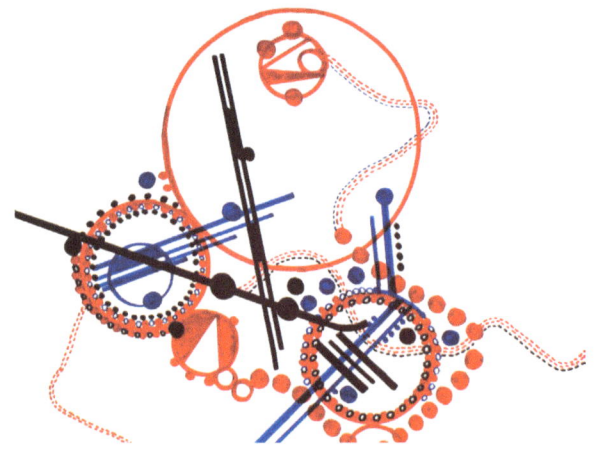

Dr. Ginger Lai was born and raised in Taipei, Taiwan. She immigrated to the US when she was sixteen years old and currently resides in Los Angeles, California. Her artwork has been on display in a variety of venues including shows at the Sasse Museum of Art in Los Angeles and The Art of Adorning show at the Bowers Museum in Orange County, CA. Dr. Lai is a doctor of clinical psychology, having earned a bachelor's degree in psychology from the University of Southern California in Los Angeles and a doctorate in clinical psychology from Pepperdine University in Malibu, California. In 2003 she launched the Gingi™ Cellular Revitalizing system, the first skincare product of its kind combining the worlds of water filtration and skincare, with the finest ingredients and purest water. Gingi™ products having been selected as official gifts for presenters of Hollywood's prestigious Academy Awards®, Emmy® and Grammy® Awards. Today, Dr. Lai integrates her therapy background in her art design and jewelry, to suit the best of visual perceptions, creating art and jewelry that can be appreciated and worn by anyone seeking to engage with a unique expression to the world around us.

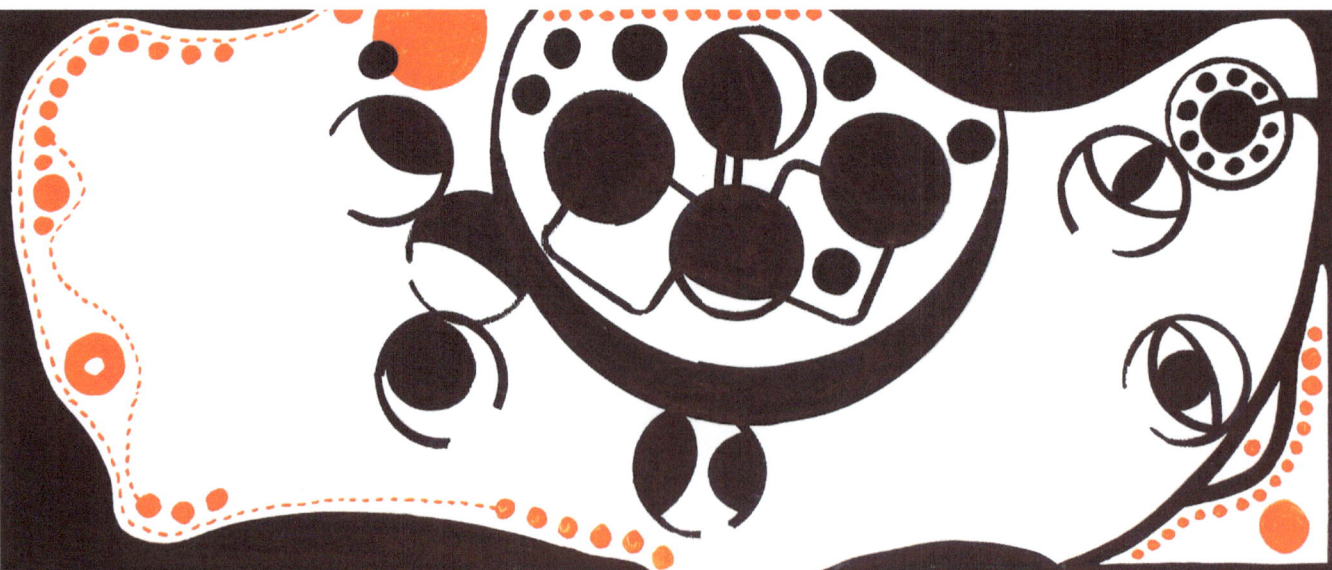

213-373-4361 - www.artsofpoetry.com - artsofpoetry@gmail.com

Ginger Lai - Sacred Geometry

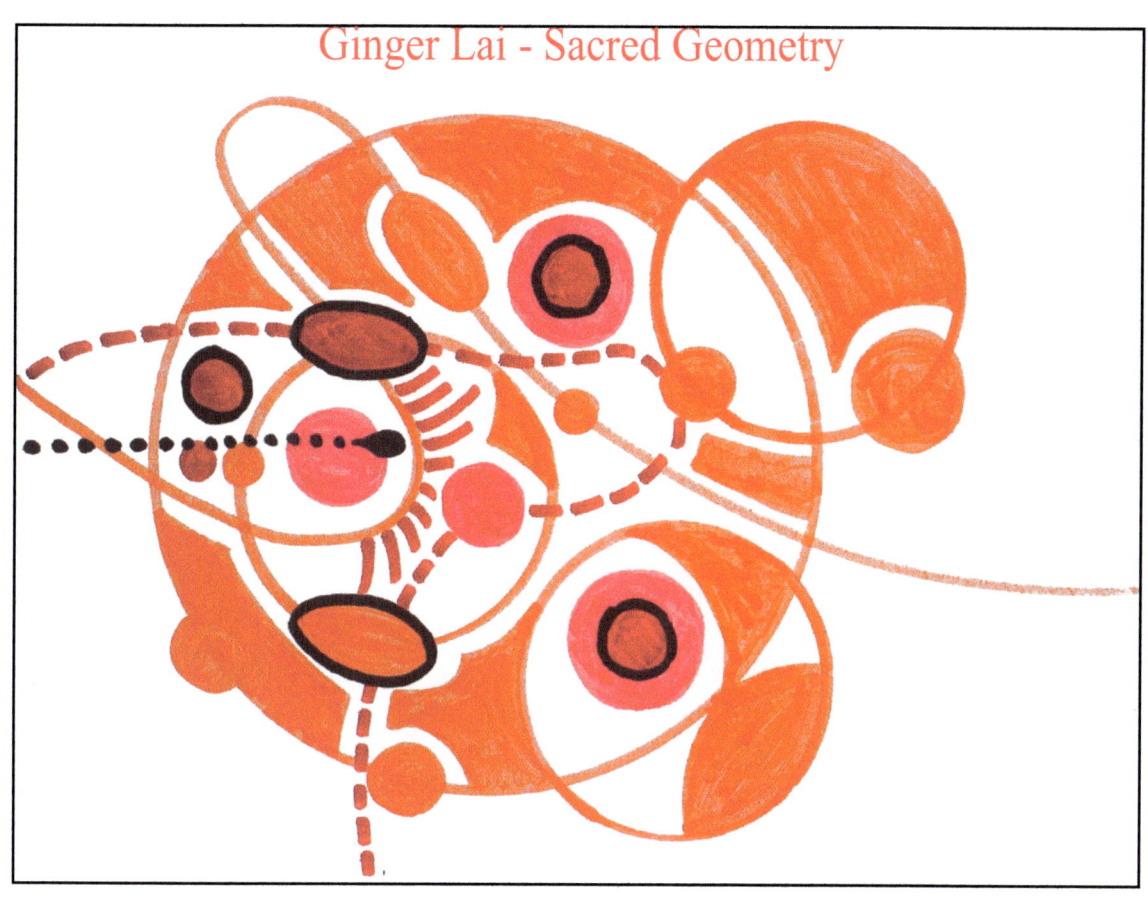

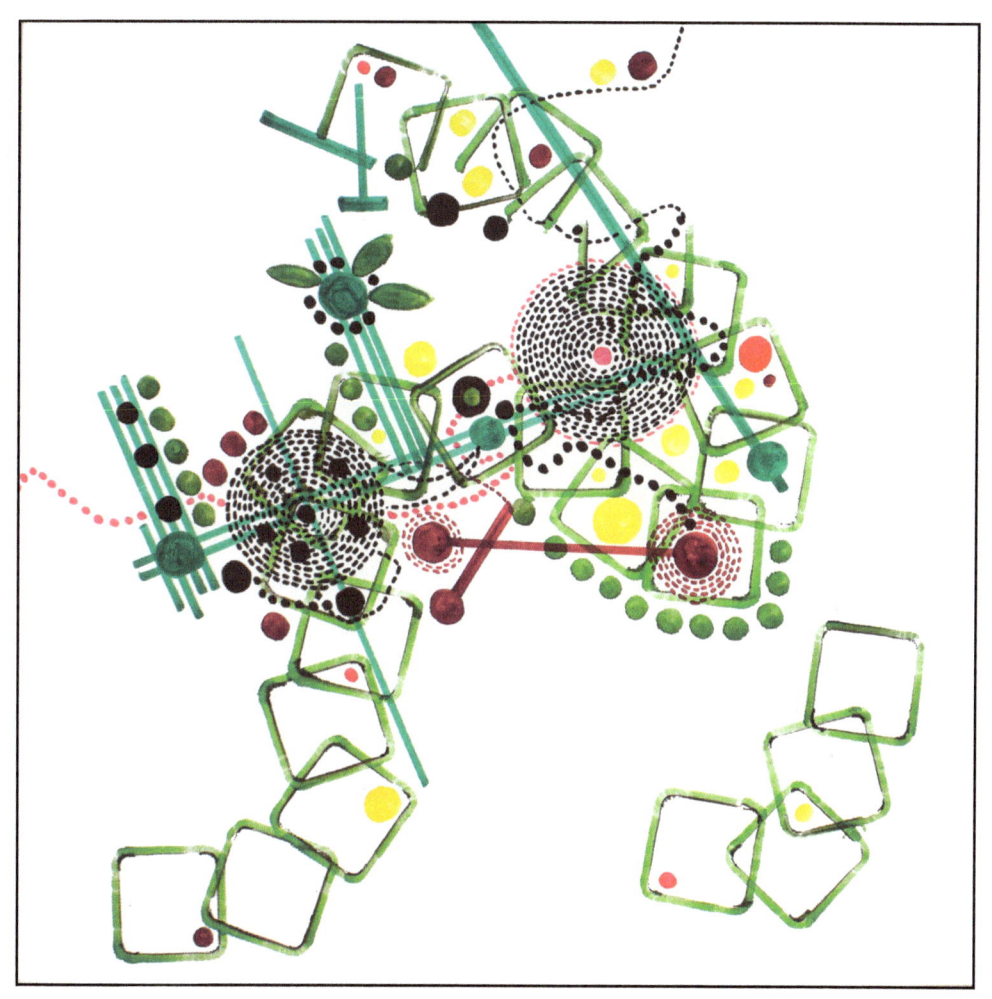

213-373-4361 - www.artsofpoetry.com - artsofpoetry@gmail.com

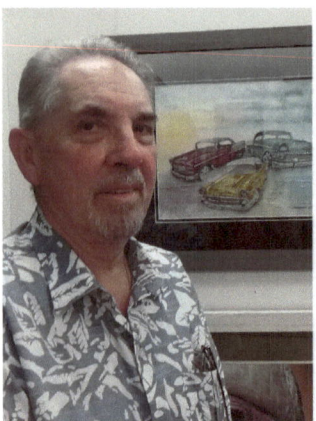

Jim Balderrama

Undersea turtle titled "TORTUGA" Done in watercolor, from the Florida keys.

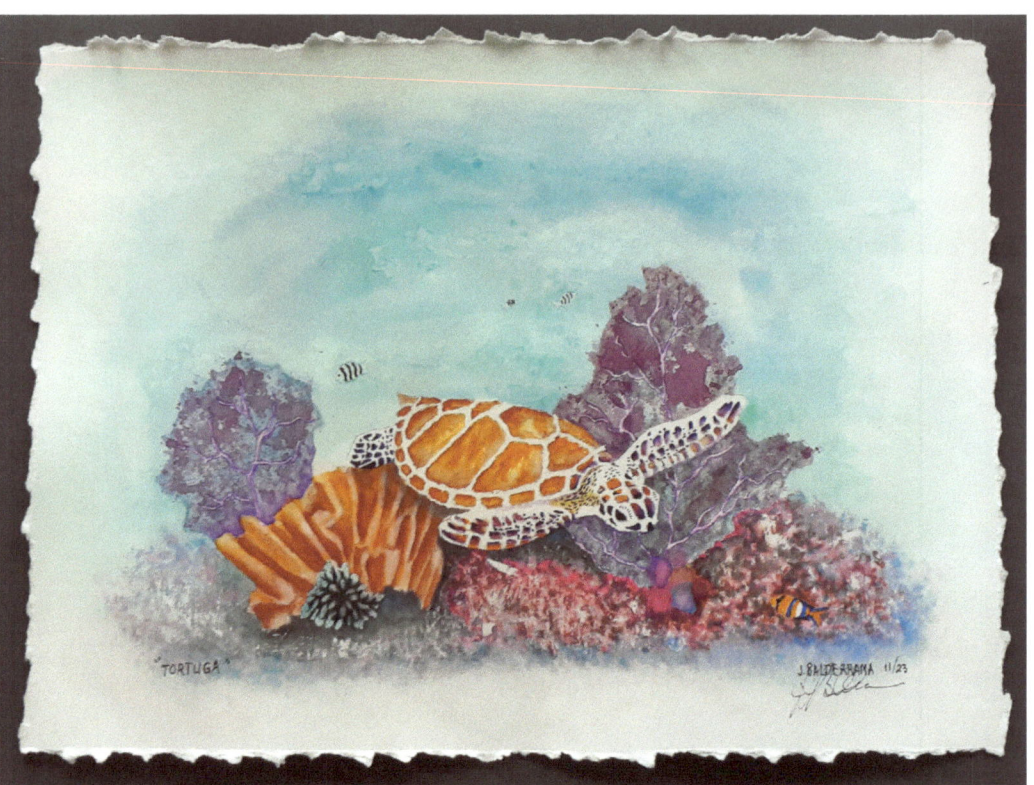

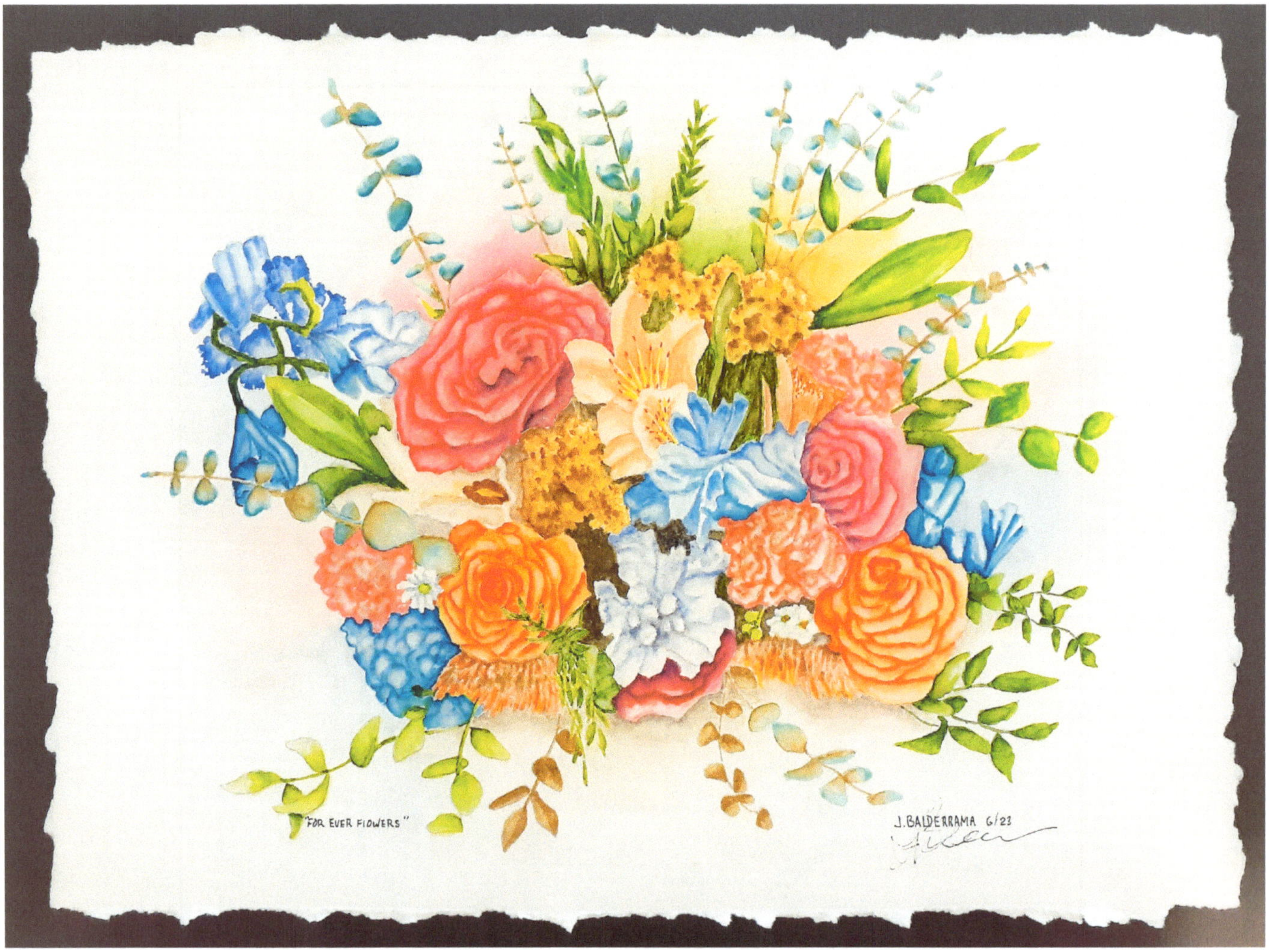

" FOREVER FLOWERS " PAINTED IN watercolor, FOREVER because these will never wilt and die

213-373-4361 - www.artsofpoetry.com - artsofpoetry@gmail.com

Monrovia Association of Fine Arts

The gathering was treated to the ethereal magic of the String Quartet from Pasadena Youth Symphony Orchestra. They wowed the crowd with their masterful renditions of classical and modern romantic music. Seriously, you should have been there--It was magic. Many thanks to MAFA member Bill Shieff for arranging their visit with us for the whole afternoon. Sally Weiss and 10 adults created portraits of their favorite pets. It was fun to do and the results were amazing.

These middle school students won prizes in the student art competition: Clifton Middle School and Santa Fe School. Rivanis Baking Company donated a delicious spread of winter weather treats and hors d'oeuvres... and Wine of the Month Club donated the adult beverages.

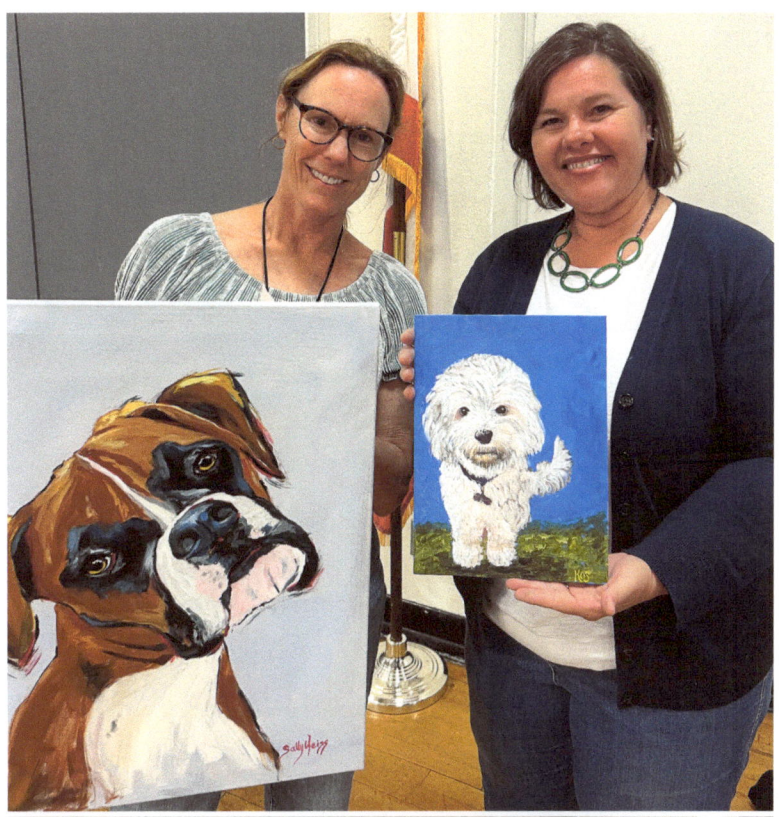

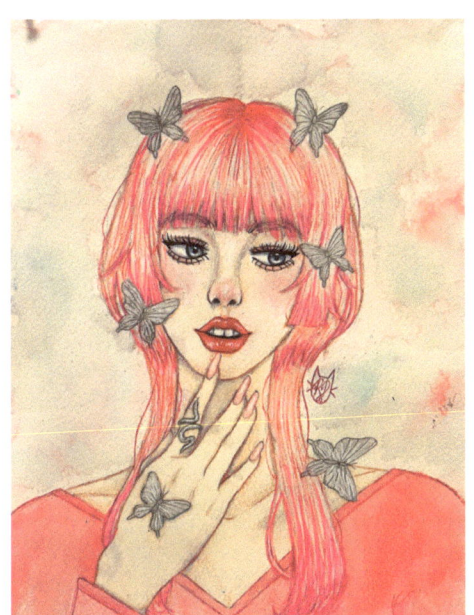

Clifton Middle School, Second Place: Rachael DeGuzman

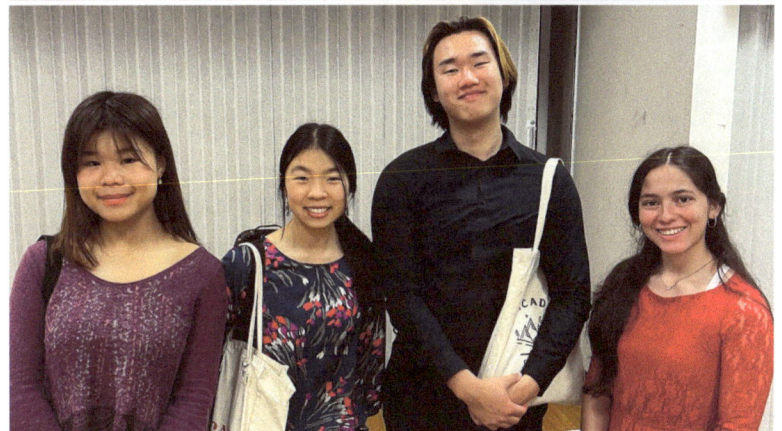

String Quartet from Pasadena Youth Symphony Orchestra

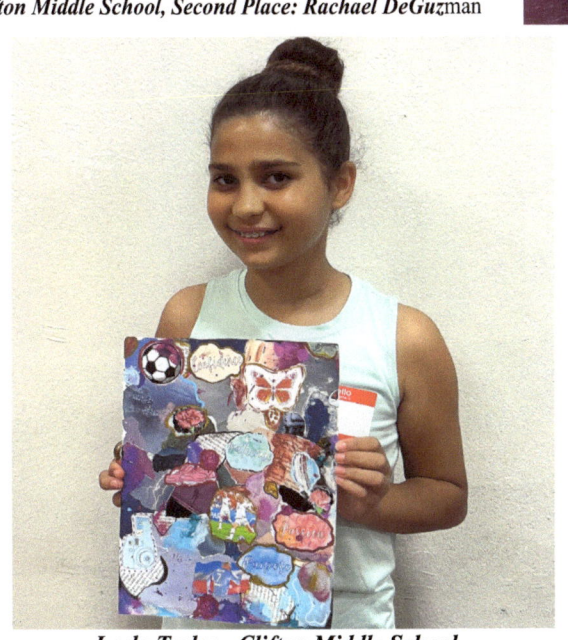

Leela Taylor - Clifton Middle School

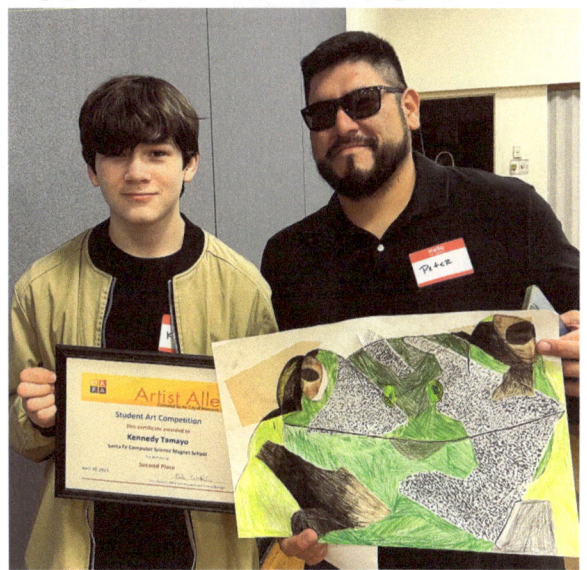

Santa Fe School Second Place: Kenney Tamayo

213-373-4361 - www.artsofpoetry.com - artsofpoetry@gmail.com

Dan Frembling

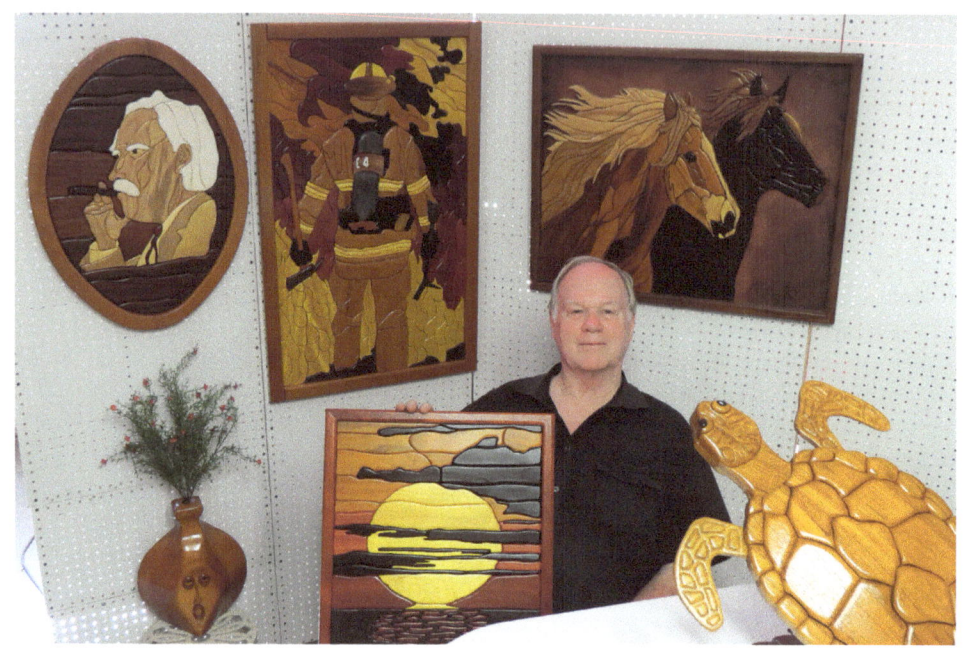

MUSTARD CHESHIRE CAT

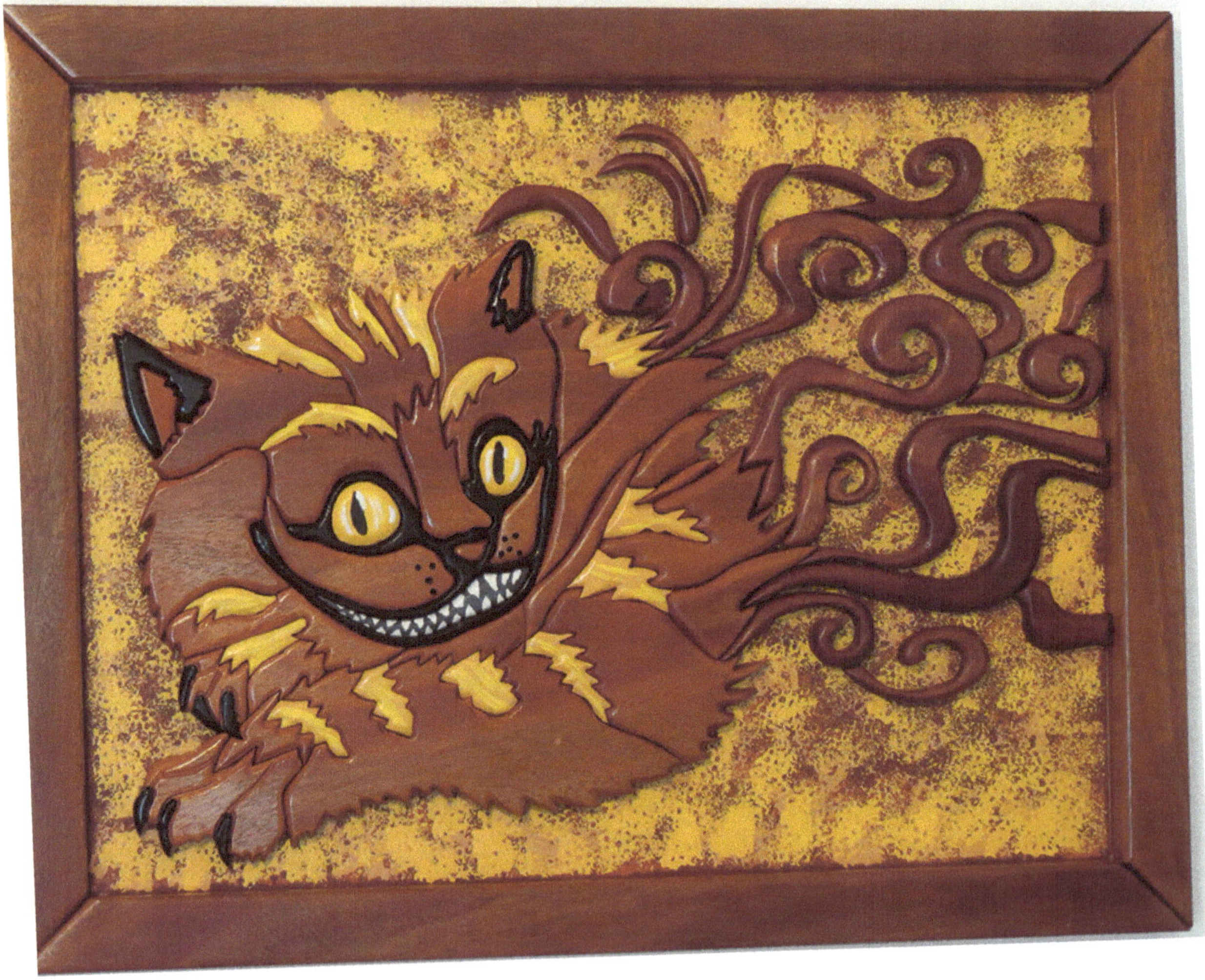

213-373-4361 - www.artsofpoetry.com - artsofpoetry@gmail.com

Dan Frembling

Inspiration for Art can strike at any moment, be ready for it.

It is an enormous sense of fulfillment and accomplishment to create something that is appreciated and desired by someone else. Many of my works are currently displayed at the Chaffee Community Museum of Art

frembling@verizon.net - DanFrembling.com

CHRISTAS SUNSET

ADVENTURE & TREASURE

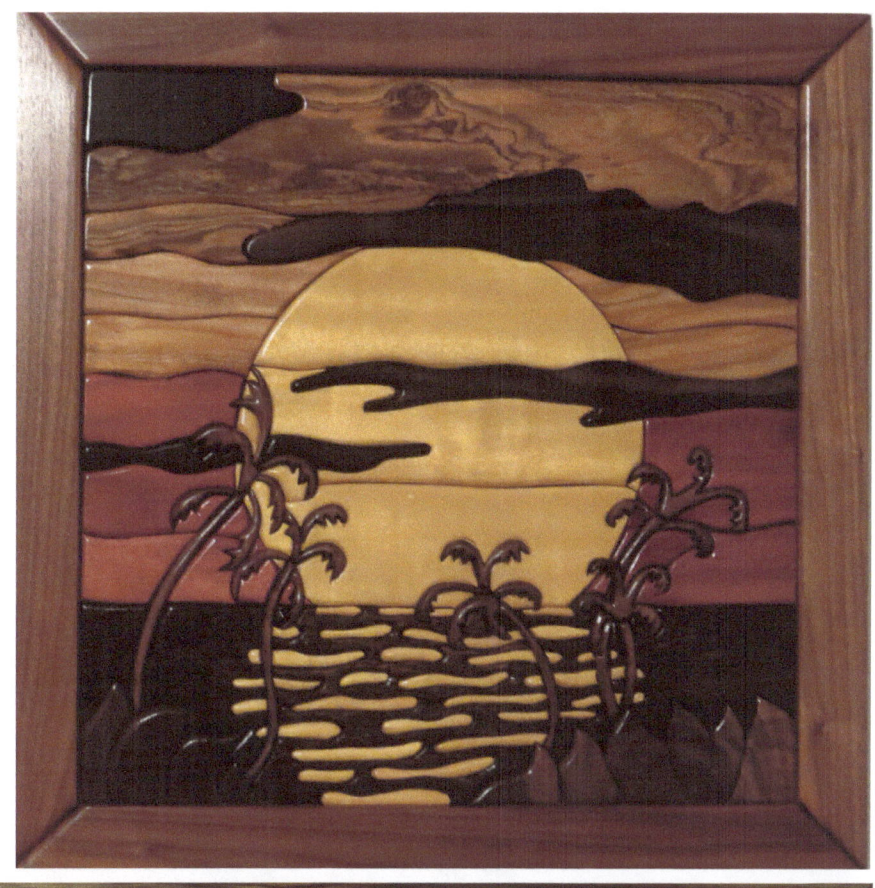

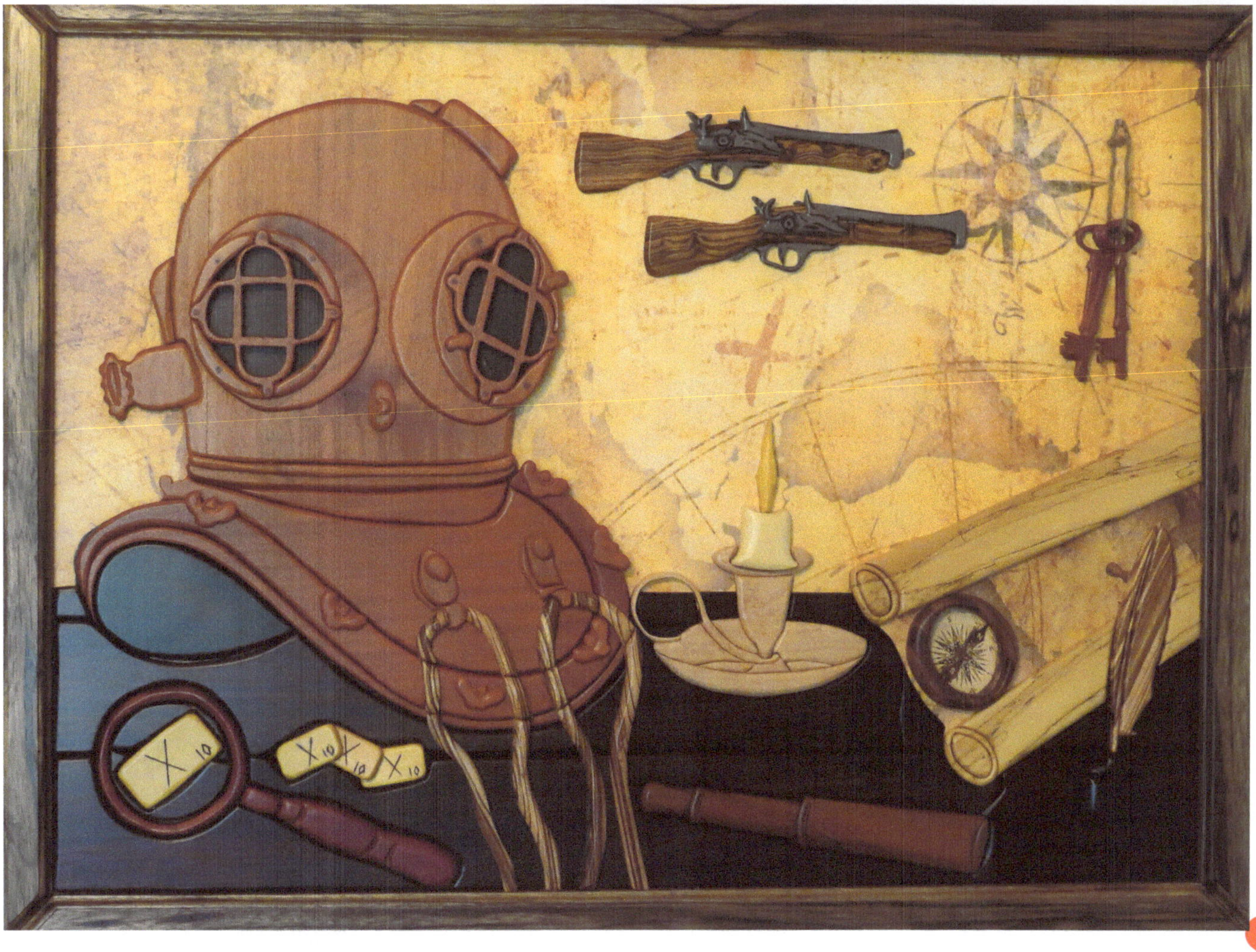

213-373-4361 - www.artsofpoetry.com - artsofpoetry@gmail.com

The Saturday Evening POST

October 21, 1950   15¢

Rockwell' THE COIN TOSS

www.ingramcontent.com/pod-product-compliance
Lightning Source LLC
Chambersburg PA
CBHW051823210526
45473CB00005B/1711